MULTICULTURAL STUDIO ART PROJECTS
FOR SECONDARY STUDENTS

Ready-to-Use Lesson Plans,
Color Prints and Worksheets
for Exploring Eight
World Cultures

SUSAN HOGAN

Pearson
Education

PRENTICE HALL
Paramus, NJ 07652

Library of Congress Cataloging-in-Publication Data

Hogan, Susan.
    Multicultural studio art projects for secondary students / Susan Hogan.
    p.   cm.
    Includes bibliographical references.
    ISBN 0-13-287442-3
    1. Art—Study and teaching (Secondary)—United States. 2. Art—Study and teaching
(Secondary)—Activity programs. 3. Multicultural education.   I. Title.
    N350.H55   1997
    707.1'273—dc21   97-12788
                                                                                          CIP

Printed in the United States of America

10 9 8 7 6 5 4 3 2 1

ISBN 0-13-287442-3

ATTENTION: CORPORATIONS AND SCHOOLS

Prentice Hall books are available at quantity discounts with bulk purchase for educational, business, or sales promotional use. For information, please write to: Prentice Hall Career & Personal Development Special Sales, 240 Frisch Court, Paramus, New Jersey 07652. Please supply: title of book, ISBN, quantity, how the book will be used, date needed.

PRENTICE HALL
Career & Personal Development
Paramus, NJ 07652
A Simon & Schuster Company

On the World Wide Web at http://www.phdirect.com

Prentice Hall International (UK) Limited, *London*
Prentice Hall of Australia Pty. Limited, *Sydney*
Prentice Hall Canada, Inc., *Toronto*
Prentice Hall Hispanoamericana, S.A., *Mexico*
Prentice Hall of India Private Limited, *New Delhi*
Prentice Hall of Japan, Inc., *Tokyo*
Simon & Schuster Asia Pte. Ltd., *Singapore*
Editora Prentice Hall do Brasil, Ltda., *Rio de Janeiro*

Dedicated to the many thousands of artisans
whose anonymous handwork continues to transmit
the inspiration that has generated the heart of this book.

ABOUT THE AUTHOR

Susan Hogan received a Master of Education degree in Art and Art Education at Teachers College, Columbia University. Ms. Hogan participated extensively as an artist-in-residence in the public schools of New York City, and taught art and social studies at Harbor School for the Performing Arts in East Harlem. She has taught courses in design, drawing, painting, collage, ceramics, and art education at William Paterson College, Caldwell College, the Newark Museum Arts Workshop, and Old Church Cultural Center Art School.

She earned an MFA in painting from Louisiana State University. Her work has been included in exhibits at the National Museum of Women in Arts, the Museum of New Mexico, the Montclair Art Museum, the Morris Museum, and the Noyes Museum. Her exhibition record of mixed media paintings includes twelve one-person shows.

As a mixed media artist, Ms. Hogan has welcomed many opportunities to develop different applications of visual art. Her various freelance artforms have included design development for fantasy films (Jim Henson Associates and Tony Walton), construction of props and puppets for movies and television (Jim Henson Associates and Astoria Film Studios), creative sculpture for dance companies and opera (Novantiqua, Candice Christakos Dancers, and Santa Fe Opera), and scenic art for student and regional theater as well as photography, ceramic sculpture, and art furniture. She was awarded a Visual Arts Fellowship in Mixed Media by the New Jersey State Council of the Arts.

ABOUT THIS BOOK

Art teachers in grades 7 through 12, as well as teachers of academic subjects who want to make their lessons tangible and visible, will find abundant new material in this resource manual. These 44 studio art projects present imaginative ways to interpret traditional art forms, based on specific cultural content. They present a fresh approach to hands-on assignments in collage and decoupage, clay, mosaic, carving in wood and plaster, painting, jewelry, and metal work, as well as some new ideas for using materials, such as dry media on carpet and sculpting in Styrofoam.

Each of these ready-to-use lesson plans is presented within a brief context of historical and geographical information that will engage the interest of your students. Thirty color plates are included in the abundant visual material provided to support the lessons. At least one pictorial resource is given for each studio art project, and a photo of each completed project is included as well, to help you visualize some of the many possibilities for a final product.

A creative writing activity is suggested at the conclusion of each hands-on project. Reproducible student worksheets for vocabulary and geography are provided for each section. A list of related assignments suggests ways to extend the stimulation of doing the artwork to the study of history, literature, human rights, international trade, current events, and more.

For many of the eight world cultures covered in this book, typical design motifs are included to provide a starting point for student work. Traditional artisans always served an apprenticeship working from prototypes to develop both skill and content in their chosen art. Byzantine mosaics in Turkey, tankas in Tibet, and metalwork in Ireland are just a few examples in this book of brilliant art forms grounded in a centuries-long visual vocabulary of images. Studying the way in which cultural information is transmitted in practical art forms contributes to understanding the meaning of distinctive historic styles. It also provides the visual information to stimulate the students' own imaginative development.

Your students will learn basic principles of design in doing these projects, as well as the vocabulary of art. This hands-on design instruction promotes not only awareness of the universal human role as producer of material things, but also the way this material production expresses human relationships: to one another and to particular places and events.

Social context and gender roles in art production will be of particular interest to adolescent students as they consider the ways in which art develops personal identity and functions to convey community values. Local, national, and global economics of trade based on the production and consumption of artwork can be researched, and studying the sources of raw materials for all of these arts will encourage environmental awareness.

Most of these different studio art projects could be pursued in several directions:

- *Creative expression:* Use any particular project, whether in collage, relief sculpture, costume, or mosaic, as the introduction for more personal creative exploration of the material and process.

- *Specific skills:* Jewelry design (Projects 5-4, 5-5, and 6-4) and woodcarving (Project 5-6) are examples of projects that could be varied and repeated to develop and refine certain craft abilities.

- *Subject areas:* More comprehensive study of Chinese architecture, for example, could follow Project 8-3; similarly, Project 1-2 (the timeline painting) could introduce in-depth coverage of ancient history in Asia Minor.

Most of these studio projects, although presented here in a specific cultural context, could be transferred to many other areas. For example:

- *map collages* (Mali)—develop for any country or region
- *timeline paintings* (Turkey)—use to depict any historic events
- *resort hotel collage* (Turkey)—situate in any country
- *landscape painting from photos* (Ireland)—use to study any geography
- *heraldry* (Ireland)—transfer to Germany, France, or England
- *"stained" glass* (Ireland)—develop for France, England, or America
- *pagodas* (China)—apply to Southeast Asia, Korea, or Japan
- *shoes* (China)—transfer to most other cultures and histories
- *costume studies* (India and China)—transfer to most other cultures
- *jewelry* (Mali and India)—apply to most other cultures
- *architectural relief sculpture* (Hopi)—use for all of the Americas, Africa, Central Asia including Tibet, and India
- *clay vessels* and *artifacts* (Hopi, Maya, and China)—can be almost universally applied in cultural studies

The materials listed for each studio art project are easily available, or can be ordered from school art supply catalogs. Whether your budget is small or huge, recycling the abundance of extra "stuff" that is habitually wasted in contemporary life into student art teaches economy and resourcefulness, and encourages students to look at the world around them with a view to transforming it. Some free or very cheap materials that you may find readily available include:

- corrugated cardboard cartons
- cloth
- carpet remnants and samples
- food packaging—cereal and cracker boxes
- plastic liter bottles
- printed advertising brochures
- disposable aluminum pans
- clay/earth
- sand
- wood—bark and logs in nature, scraps from construction
- windows
- feathers

Becoming familiar with materials and processes can generate a flood of new ideas and possibilities for student work. Using free materials particularly confers the freedom to experiment and explore. I hope these ideas in these accessible procedures ignite compelling new connections for you, and open up promising new directions in curriculum integration. Most of all, I wish you the sheer fun of actually doing all these things!

Susan Hogan

ACKNOWLEDGMENTS

I am truly thankful to everyone who so generously offered their enthusiastic support in developing these projects, helping with research, and making the right pictures available. Your interest, time, and energy have been most important in bringing this project to completion, and are most gratefully appreciated.

For their vital contributions to the section on Turkey, appreciation goes to Howard and Suzanne Berelson for taking photographs throughout their trip. To Howard, I am also indebted for the concept of the face tickets, and to the ceramic students at Caldwell College for their little clay sketches of faces. I greatly appreciate the cooperation of H̄useyin Aktuḡ in permitting me to photograph the imported kilims and mosaic tabletops in his shop, Istanbul Grand Bazaar. Thanks to Paul and Phyllis Kronick for my first visual tour of Turkey via their slides, and for the long-term loan of their books. Kevin Radcliffe of Pacha Tours was most helpful in making their extensive slide file available to me.

For the Ireland section, Marjorie Shaw Kubach generously allowed me to include her watercolors of Irish landscapes and photographs of Irish castles. Orla Carie at the Irish Tourist Board provided the photographs of the stone heraldic emblem. Thanks to Charlie McGill for the long-term loan of his books on Ireland.

For the Hopi section, Kathy Butterly's support for the clay projects was vital. Many photographs of Nampeyo pottery and contemporary kachina dolls were generously given to me by the Penfield Gallery in Albuquerque. Charles and Leslie Donaldson of Scottsdale graciously helped me to photograph their antique kachina dolls. Thanks to Arthur L. Olivas at the Museum of New Mexico for his rapid response to my request for the photographs of Hopi mesas and of the Butterfly Dance. Robert W. Rhodes of Sonwai in Hotevilla provided an extensive bibliography on Hopi art.

In the section on the Maya, many of the photos of Mayan architecture were provided by my father, Zebulon W. White. Kathy Butterly contributed her artistic and technical expertise to the development of the clay projects. The sculpted face of Magdalena Krekora appears on the Mayan portrait pot. Bea Colao referred me to the Lands Beyond gallery in New York City, where Kenneth Bowers graciously helped me to photograph the Mayan cylinder vases and Jaina figurines. Clinton Taplin offered his slides of Mayan women weaving, and Denise Charlot of the Guatemalan Trade Commission also contributed slides of Mayan weaving.

For the section on Mali, my thanks and appreciation to Mana Diakite, who was so generous in sharing his personal knowledge of African life and his collection of the arts of Mali to be photographed. Thanks also to Anique Taylor and Virginia Cornue for their enthusiastic participation in developing the African trade bead project, and to Ruth Neustadter for collaborating with me on the Tuareg-inspired leather bag. Arnold Syrop generously provided the photograph of the unique carved Dogon granary door. Ed Johnson of the African Art Museum in Tenafly offered new insight into Dogon sculpture, and assistance in photographing the masks.

For the India section, many thanks are due to Marguerite Botto, Beverly Fuchsman, and Mary Anne Rich for helping develop the appliquéd vest project and the collage bangles. Lauraine Schallop at Air India was most helpful in providing the slides of Indian women and costumed painted elephants. Thanks to Anique Taylor for creating paintings on pavement, and grateful appreciation for her support and encouragement throughout. Kathy Butterly made a special effort to photograph the rangolis for me in southern India, and thanks as well to Penny and David Dell for lending me their paintings from India.

For Tibet, Valrae Reynolds of the Newark Museum offered me important insight into Tibetan art and knowledgeable assistance in obtaining appropriate pictures from the Newark Museum's collection. Michael Knowlton at Inner Asia Trading Company generously provided the quality color slides of contemporary Tibetan carpets.

For the section on China, great appreciation to Virginia Cornue for offering me her scholar's perspective on life in contemporary China, as well as continual enthusiasm, interest, and support for this entire undertaking. Thanks to Ron Hollander for the stories and videos of travel in China, and for his professional perspective on the work of writing. Thanks again to Valrae Reynolds for her assistance with obtaining photographs of Chinese art from the Newark Museum's collection, as well as for her enthusiasm for the project. I am grateful to Marguerite Botto and Beverly Fuchsman for allowing me to include their interpretations of the Chinese costume collage project, and to Jade Garden Arts and Crafts Co. for permitting me to photograph the jade mountain sculpture.

For designing and producing the map graphics that accompany each section, thanks to my husband, Bill Hogan. Finally, profound gratitude to Bill for patiently enduring the entire span of evolution of this book.

CONTENTS

About This Book   vii

SECTION ONE
TURKEY
1

A Brief History of Turkey   2

Turkey Was a Greek Colony   3
    Project 1-1: Making Molded Clay Faces   5

Turkish Archaeology   6
    Project 1-2: Painting a Timeline of Turkish History   6

Mosaic Art of Asia Minor and Byzantium   13
    Project 1-3: Making a Mosaic Tabletop   14

Turkish Tile Art   16
    Project 1-4: Making Glazed Star Tiles   17

Turkish Kilims   22
    Project 1-5: Making Colored Drawings of Kilims on Cloth   25
    Project 1-6: Collage of Hotel Room Decorated with Kilims   29

Vocabulary Worksheet for Turkey   33

Geography Worksheet for Turkey   34

Related Assignments for Turkey   36

Resources for Teaching   37

Bibliography   37

SECTION TWO

IRELAND
39

A Brief History of Ireland   40

    Project 2-1: Painting Irish Landscape from Photographs   42

Irish Stone Structures   45

    Project 2-2: Making a Stone Collage Castle   48

Irish Artistry in Metal   49

    Project 2-3: Making an Embossed Brass Book Cover   50

Stained Glass in Ireland   55

    Project 2-4: Painting on Glass (or Plexiglas ™)   55

Heraldry in Ireland   60

    Project 2-5: Carving a Heraldic Emblem in Clay   63

Vocabulary Worksheet for Ireland   67

Geography Worksheet for Ireland   68

Related Assignments for Ireland   70

Resources for Teaching   71

Bibliography   72

SECTION THREE

SOUTHWEST AMERICA: THE HOPI
73

A Brief History of the Hopi   74

Working with Clay   76

Making Pottery in the Hopi Style   77

    Project 3-1: Forming Clay Bowls in Press Molds   77

Project 3-2: Forming Hopi-style Coil Pots 79
Project 3-3: Making a Hopi Canteen 82

Hopi Mesas and Villages 85

Project 3-4: Sculpting a Clay Relief of Mesa-top Villages 86

Hopi Silverwork 89

Project 3-5: Making Aluminum Concha Belts in Hopi Style 90

Hopi Kachinas 94

Project 3-6: Making a Folio of Kachina Drawings 97

Tablitas: Headdresses for Ceremonial and Social Dances 98

Project 3-7: Making Painted Tablitas Cut Out of Foam Core 102

Vocabulary Worksheet for the Hopi 107

Geography Worksheet for the Hopi 108

Related Assignments for the Hopi 109

Resources for Teaching 110

Bibliography 111

SECTION FOUR

CENTRAL AMERICA: THE MAYA
113

A Brief History of the Maya 114

Mayan Architecture 116

Project 4-1: Sculpting a Mayan Mask Facade 118

Mayan Relief Sculpture 121

Project 4-2: Making a Mayan Self-portrait Pot 121

Mayan Cylindrical Clay Vessels 127

Project 4-3: Making a Painted Clay Cylinder Vase 127

Mayan Figurines from Jaina 130

Project 4-4: Making a Mayan Goddess Rattle 130

Mayan Weaving 134
Project 4-5: Weaving a Mat on a Cardboard Loom 135

Vocabulary Worksheet for the Maya 138

Geography Worksheet for the Maya 141

Related Assignments for the Maya 143

Resources for Teaching 144

Bibliography 145

SECTION FIVE

MALI
147

A Brief History of Mali 148
Project 5-1: Map Painting 149

The Bambara People of Central Mali 150
Project 5-2: Chi Wara Carving 150

The Tuareg People of the Northern Desert 156
Project 5-3: Making a Tuareg-style Leather Bag 159

The Fulani People of the Niger Delta 162
Project 5-4: Making African Trade Beads of Polymer Clay 165
Project 5-5: Stringing African-inspired Necklaces 166

The Dogon People of the Bandiagara Cliffs in Southeast Mali 170
Project 5-6: Dogon Woodcarving 173
Project 5-7: Mali Map Collage Painting 174

Vocabulary Worksheet for Mali 176

Geography Worksheet for Mali 177

Related Assignments for Mali 179

Resources for Teaching 180

Bibliography 180

S ECTION S IX

INDIA
183

A Brief History of India 184

Elephants in Indian Life and Art 187
   Project 6-1: Carving an Elephant Bas-relief in Plaster   189

Textile Arts of Village India 190
   Project 6-2: Making a Mixed Media Collage Vest   191

Jewelry in Ancient and Modern India 192
   Project 6-3: Making a Jewelry Collage   199
   Project 6-4: Making Découpage Arm Bangles   203

Painted Homes of Village India 203
   Project 6-5: Painting on Sidewalks and Parking Lots   203

Vocabulary Worksheet for India 208

Geography Worksheet for India 209

Related Assignments for India 211

Resources for Teaching 212

Bibliography 213

S ECTION S EVEN

TIBET
215

A Brief History of Tibet 216

Tibetan Buddhism 217

Tibetan Tankas 219
   Project 7-1: Painting an Ideal World   220

Tibetan Ceremonial Instruments   224

Project 7-2: Making a Tibetan Skull Drum   224

Tibetan Carpets   227

Project 7-3: Painting a Tibetan Tiger Rug   229

Metalworking Traditions in Tibet   233

Project 7-4: Making a Copper Repoussé Plaque   234
Project 7-5: Making a Copper Repoussé Amulet Box   238

Vocabulary Worksheet for Tibet   242

Geography Worksheet for Tibet   243

Related Assignments for Tibet   245

Resources for Teaching   246

Bibliography   247

SECTION EIGHT

CHINA
249

A Brief History of China   250

Chinese Jade   251

Project 8-1: Making "Jade" Pendants and Medallions
     Out of Polymer Clay   252

Chinese Porcelain   258

Project 8-2: Making a Chinese Moon Flask   261

Chinese Pagodas   263

Project 8-3: Building a Model Watchtower Out of Clay   264

Chinese Costumes   266

Project 8-4: Making a Fabric Collage of Historical
     Chinese Costumes   269

Chinese Shoes of Cotton Cloth   271
 Project 8-5: Making Appliquéd Slippers 271

Vocabulary Worksheet for China   279

Geography Worksheet for China   280

Related Assignments for China   282

Resources for Teaching   283

Bibliography   283

SECTION ONE
Turkey

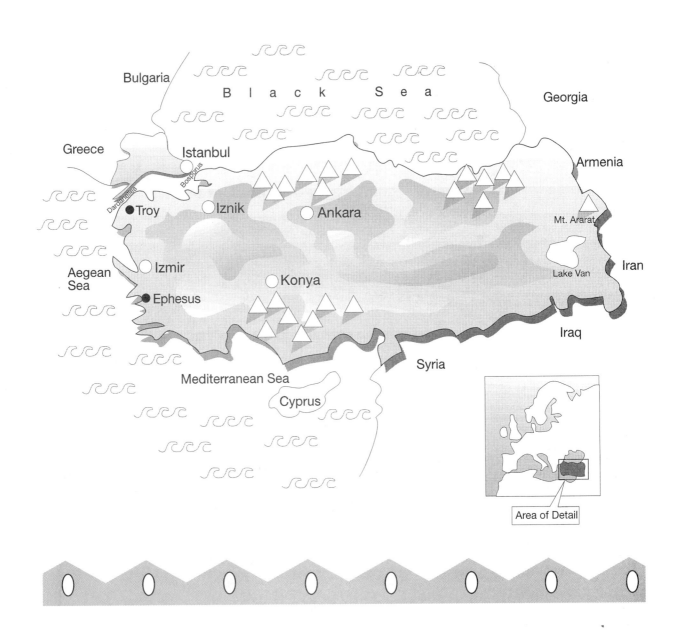

A BRIEF HISTORY OF TURKEY

The Republic of Turkey is strategically situated at the juncture of Europe, the Middle East, and Asia. (See Figure 1–1.) Nine-tenths of the country is in Asia, occupying a peninsula that juts out in a western direction, bounded on three sides by water: the Mediterranean on the south side, the Aegean Sea on the west, and the Black Sea on the north. In its long and tumultuous history, Turkey has been identified as the Hittite civilization, the Persian Empire, Magna Graecia, the Roman Empire, Asia Minor, the Byzantine Empire, the Seljuk Sultanates, the Ottoman Empire, and Anatolia by the succession of peoples who have occupied this land since Catal Hoyuk, the earliest known human settlement was established here around 6250 B.C.

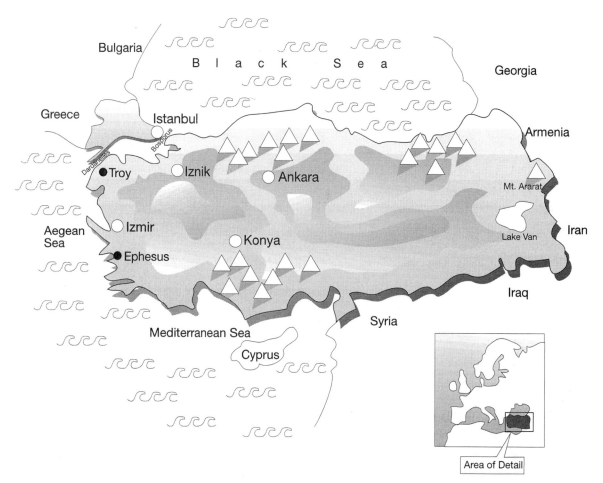

Figure 1-1. Map of Turkey. This is a simplified locator map for quick reference. Students can look up a more detailed map of Turkey in a world atlas.

Turkey's largest metropolis, Istanbul, is the ancient port city of the Golden Horn, the best natural harbor in the Eastern Mediterranean. From its origin as Byzantium in 667 B.C., the city was renamed Constantinople, the Roman capital of the Byzantine Empire, in the year 326. When the Ottoman Turks captured the city in 1453, they renamed it Istanbul, or city of the mosque, to express the triumph of Islam over Christianity. Heiress to a magnificent architectural heritage built by the succession of Byzantine, Roman, and Ottoman rulers, Istanbul and its suburbs on both sides of the Bosporus are now home to about 11 million people. Recent urban development initiatives to return the metropolis to its former world-class status have included constructing massive new highways, water supply systems, and sewer systems. This large-scale renovation of infrastructure has come into conflict with historic preservation of the city's cultural heritage.

New subway systems have been built in spite of the constant discovery of archaeological artifacts from the city's past. Two elegant new suspension bridges span the Bosporus, the narrow and turbulent waterway from the Black Sea into the Sea of Marmora, the Dardanelles, and the eastern Mediterranean. This route is Russia's only link between its warm-water ports on the Black Sea for oil tankers from which its vast oil reserves are shipped out to world markets.

Turkey was established as a modern republic by Ataturk, the national hero, in 1923. The nation has been engaged in a balancing act between its Muslim identification (99% of the people are Muslims) with the Arab countries of the Middle East, and its desire to be included in the liberal democratic and economic traditions of Western Europe.

TURKEY WAS A GREEK COLONY

'Turkuaz' (turquoise) is the Turkish word that describes the intense blue-green color of the Aegean and Mediterranean waters. All along Turkey's Aegean coast can be found many many ruins of Greek and Roman cities. Ancient Greeks fled south to Anatolia some time between the thirteenth and twelfth centuries B.C., when their country was invaded by armies from the north. They built cities just like those they had left behind, with a central *agora*, or marketplace, law courts, municipal buildings, theater and temples, and an orderly grid of streets. These new cities of Magna Graecia shared the language, culture, and democratic tradition of mainland Greece.

Today the ruins of these cities of antiquity are a very popular tourist destination. It is said that more art and artifacts of ancient Greece are still visible here than in Greece itself. Pergamum in particular still has a wealth of Greek and Roman remains, including ruins of the great library, a temple of Athena, and a restored theater. (See Figure 1–2.)

The ancient city of Aphrodisias was dedicated to the goddess of love, and known as a center for sculpture. The Temple of Aphrodite, although later converted to a Christian basilica, is very well preserved. A museum at the site displays portrait sculptures and statues in the distinctive style of this city.

Priene was an important commercial seaport around 300 B.C., until its harbor slowly silted up over the centuries. The ruins of Priene, originally laid out in a grid by King Mausolos in 350 B.C., are now ten miles from the sea. Remains of the Temple of Athena, the Council House, and a 6,000-seat theater are evidence of civic life devoted to sports, culture, and the gods.

The large amphitheaters constructed in Greek times are one of the most prominent features of all of these ruins. In them were held the performances, speeches, drama, and sporting events, public rituals that strengthened community identity and bound the citizens into a common cause. The best preserved theater is at Aspendos. It has a capacity of 15,000 spectators, and is still used today for special events.

Tickets admitting the ancient Greeks to arena events were in the form of little faces molded of clay. (See Figure 1–3.) Different seating locations were signified by different types of faces. These coin-size clay faces that were used as tickets in the Greek cities of the Anatolian coast are directly related to the first metal coinage, which originated in nearby Lydia.

Figure 1-2. Remains of an ancient amphitheater that was built into a hillside with panoramic views. (Photograph by Suzanne Berelson.)

Figure 1-3. Tickets for the show: small (1-inch) replicas of authentic artifacts from ancient Greek amphitheaters on the Turkuaz coast. (Photograph by Howard Berelson.)

Project 1–1: Making Molded Clay Faces

PREPARATION

Have students clip photographs of all kinds of faces from print sources and glue them into their notebooks to compile a visual resource for modeling small faces of clay.

MATERIALS

- white low-fire clay, cone 06
- electric kiln
- simple wooden tools: toothpicks, skewers, craft sticks

PROCEDURE

1. Using about a 1-inch ball of clay, flatten it into an oval shape.
2. Begin your 3-D sketch by simply pressing indentations for eyes, and lengthening the nose.
3. Refer to the pictures of faces you have collected as you gradually develop and refine the facial features of these little sculptures.
4. Add stylized hair with the sharp wooden tool.
5. These sketches are fast enough so that you can make several.
6. When the little faces are thoroughly dry, fire them to cone 06.
7. "Mass produce" your face tickets by making a mold of the original. Carefully press wet clay over the fired clay face to make a negative impression of it.
8. Remove the negative mold from the original, and let it dry.
9. Fire the molds. Then you will be able to press as many fresh wet clay faces in your own face molds as you can use.

CONCLUSION

Students can exchange these mini-faces and make collections of all the different variations. See Figure 1–4 for an actual studio art project.

Figure 1-4. Studio art project. Student sketches of a wide variety of little faces.

FOLLOW-UP

- Have students examine the designs of the coins we use and consider how they may have been developed from the use of little face images as tickets. Using the clay modeling process, students can design a series of coins that also incorporate numbers and words to commemorate a particular event.

- Look at pictures of the large amphitheaters at the archaeological sites of Pergamum, Ephesus, and other cities of Asia Minor to visualize the context for large public events in ancient Greek cities. Research events that would have been staged there.

CREATIVE WRITING

Consider how tickets might have been distributed in ancient Turkey, and compare it with the way tickets for concerts and athletic events are marketed now.

TURKISH ARCHAEOLOGY

Many centuries after these cities of Magna Graecia were established, Romans took them over in their conquest of an empire spreading out around the Mediterranean. The Romans' invitation to colonize Asia Minor was extended by King Attalus III of Pergamum, the cruel, eccentric ruler who bequeathed his city to the Roman rulers upon his death in 133 B.C. Roman rule brought three hundred years of stability and prosperity to all the harbor cities of this Aegean coast. During this era, many cities of Asia Minor became scenes of Biblical history.

Ephesus was the capital of the Roman Province of Asia, and one of the five largest cities in the Roman Empire. It was at one time the wealthiest city in the Middle East. Relics from Ephesus can be dated at least as far back as 3000 B.C. Since the city was established, it was occupied by Lydians, Persians, and Greeks. In 53 A.D., Saint Paul preached in Ephesus and lived there for a short while. The Virgin Mary lived the last years of her life in Ephesus, and it was one of the seven churches to whom the Book of Revelation was addressed, at a time when Romans were still persecuting Christians.

After the seventh century, the Arabs attacked the city and destroyed much of its wealth and beauty. The Turks recaptured the remains of the city from the Byzantines in 1304 and restored prosperity, revitalizing trade and building mosques and public baths.

Touring any of these ruins, you can feel connected to centuries and centuries of the history from which the modern world has evolved. We can learn a lot about how these people lived throughout the ages from the work of archaeologists, who have carefully studied the remnants of architecture that are present here.

Archaeology is the systemic study of the material remnants of communities, cities, and civilizations of the past. Archaeologists are scholars who uncover the evidence of human history in careful excavations, and interpret their discoveries by writing theoretical reconstructions of the past.

Project 1–2: Painting a Timeline of Turkish History

The discipline of archaeology—identifying all the layers of history in one place—can be a metaphor for constructing a timeline of the varied and culturally rich civilizations that have thrived at various times in Anatolia, the land that is now Turkey. A vertical diagram of historic epochs can become the structure for a painting of the dates and words in colors to represent layers of time, creating a handsome informative picture.

PREPARATION

Students can refer to the timeline of Turkish history given here, and supplement it with more detailed information from an encyclopedia or historical atlas.

MATERIALS

- paper for watercolors, at least 18" × 24"
- crayons, colored pencils, and/or watercolor crayons
- watercolor paints and brushes
- containers for water

PROCEDURE

1. Use words and numbers as drawings. Warm up for the painting project by writing words as images with colored crayons on sketch paper.
2. When you have developed confidence in drawing bold words and numbers, make a preliminary rough layout of the placement of your time sequence on the page.
3. Using different color crayons or pencils, start at the bottom of the blank sheet of watercolor paper to write the date and name of each era of history, up to the present day at the top.
4. Paint broad washes of different colors over the words, in wide bands from bottom to top. Keep developing the layers of color to evoke looking through layers of time.
5. After the watercolor paintings dry, the words and numbers can be delineated again with the crayons, developing more intricate color layering.

CONCLUSION

Display the timeline paintings as a visible historical context during subsequent studio projects on Turkey. (See Figure 1–5 for an actual studio art project.)

FOLLOW-UP

Have students focus on just one of these historic eras to develop a word painting exploring details of a more limited time period.

CREATIVE WRITING

Choose one era of history from your painting and imagine taking a journey back through time to visit it. Visualize what you would see, how you would feel, whom you might meet, and develop the visualization in detail as you write. (*Note to Teacher:* You may want to assign this writing at the end of your study of Turkey.)

TIMELINE OF TURKISH HISTORY

Republic of Turkey	1923–present	founded by Ataturk
Ottoman Empire	1453–1922	converted Anatolia from Christianity to Islam
Seljuk Turks	1071–13th century	Sultanate of Rum
Byzantium	395 A.D.–1204	Eastern Roman Empire
Roman Empire	133 B.C.–300 A.D.	law and prosperity
Magna Graecia	12th century B.C.–133 B.C.	Greek cities on the Aegean
Alexander the Great	334 B.C.–323 B.C.	spread Hellenistic culture
Persian Empire	546 B.C.–499 B.C.	immense wealth, superb roads,
Phrygian Empire	1250 B.C.–695 B.C.	King Midas ruled from Gordion
Hittites	1800 B.C.–1200 B.C.	feudal empire, wrote cuneiform
Troy I	3000 B.C.	Bronze Age city
Catal Hoyuk	6250 B.C.	oldest known Neolithic settlement

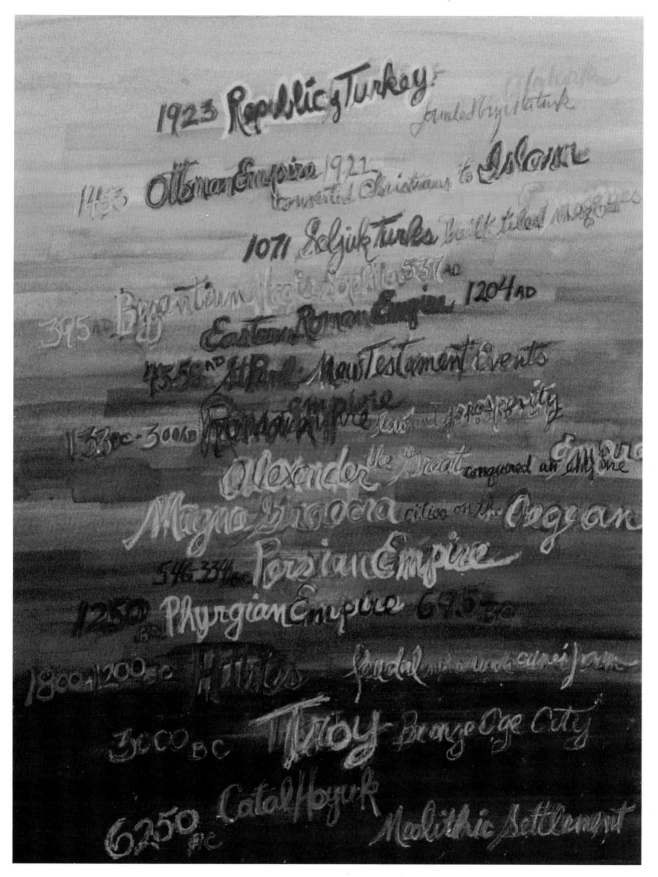

Figure 1-5. Studio art project. Dynamic and colorful words and dates impress the pattern of history on the painter's mind. (Artwork by Susan Hogan.)

Figure 1-6. Fragment of a pattern in mosaic pavement from ancient Asia Minor. (Photograph by Howard Berelson.)

MOSAIC ART OF ASIA MINOR AND BYZANTIUM

During the first century, Saint Paul preached the gospel of Christ zealously throughout the Roman province of Asia Minor. Some books of the New Testament, such as Ephesians and Timothy, are letters written by Saint Paul to congregations in different cities there. His missionary fervor must have had a far-reaching effect, because gradually all of the Roman Empire converted to Christianity. The Emperor Constantine was converted from the persecution of Christians to becoming a Christian himself. When he moved the capital city of the Roman Empire to Byzantium in 326, he changed the name of the city to reflect his own glory: it became Constantinople.

Architecture became the extension of power and authority in this newly colonized city. Constantine made massive changes and developments in the built environment, transposing Roman styles to this new center of the Eastern Roman Empire. In the sixth century, the integration of Roman and Oriental styles of architecture continued to develop, as the Emperor Justinian pursued an extensive building program of Christian basilicas, monuments of his Christian faith and of the power and wealth of his reign. Justinian dedicated the Hagia Sophia in 536 A.D.. The enormous domed basilica, the architectural wonder of Constantinople, was created by two architects from Asia Minor: Anthenius of Tralles and his assistant Isidorus of Miletus.

The Hagia Sophia became the heart and center of Byzantine Christendom throughout the centuries. The huge interior domes and walls were covered with decorative mosaic. Mosaic pictures depicting figures in Biblical scenes, especially Christ in his role as Savior of the world, were added later. The pictorial mosaic art was destroyed by iconoclasts between 729 and 843, then restored and added to in subsequent centuries. This wealth of mosaic art was rediscovered in 1933, when Ataturk made the basilica into a museum. The Ottomans had whitewashed the Christian images in 1456, when the Hagia Sophia was transformed into a mosque.

Mosaic art was a major expression of the spirit of Byzantine architecture. (See Figure 1–6.) Mosaic, defined as the use of small hard components set side by side on large surfaces, was a creation of the Greco-Roman world that became the great art form of the subsequent Byzantine Christian era. Mosaic art had been used in paving the floors and walkways, in the baths, and for developing wall and ceiling pictures in the pre-Christian Greek and Roman cities of Asia Minor. Pergamum was the center of an important school of mosaic artists.

In the many Byzantine churches of Constantinople, wall mosaics were assembled of glass tesserae, small cubes of glass that reflect light from surfaces. In the great church mosaic art, the tesserae are set at angles to glimmer and glisten in the light. They are applied over three coats of plaster; the third coat is applied in small sections, so that the components can be set into it while soft. A preliminary image was painted in full color on the setting bed as a guide to setting the mosaic. Artists worked from a catalog of conventional motifs, which they knew by heart. Their knowledge of this visual vocabulary allowed them to work directly on the wall.

During the height of the Byzantine decorative system, mosaic was used extensively in domes, apses, chapels, and on individual panels in many churches throughout the Byzantine Empire. Religious fervor was expressed in churches in Jerusalem, Kiev, Syria, Greece, and Italy. In 540, Justinian's general Belisarius captured Ravenna, which became the center of the Byzantine Empire in Italy. Full-portrait mosaics of the Emperor and his wife, Empress Theodora, standing with their courtiers, have been glowing from the walls of the church of San Vitale in Ravenna for fourteen centuries!

Project 1–3: Making A Mosaic Tabletop

Ancient pavements in Aegean cities and glittering interiors of Byzantine churches remain visible today as high points of Turkish art history. Today the mosaic heritage of Asia Minor is also evident in products designed and made in factories in Turkey for export to the home furnishings market. (See Figures 1–7A and 1–7B.)

Figures 1-7A and 1-7B. Mosaic tabletops in a variety of traditional designs are available at the Istanbul Grand Bazaar in New York City. (Courtesy of Hüseyin Aktuğ.)

Look around for available materials to use in mosaic. Save broken dishes and pottery. Have students collect flat stones, mica, shells, buttons, and miscellaneous flat materials to augment purchased glass tesserae, which can be ordered from school art supply catalogs.

PREPARATION

Pictures of Byzantine mosaics for inspiration should be readily available in art books, travel books about Istanbul, or travel brochures on Turkey. Discuss with students how ideas from these sources could be translated into sketches of design ideas for a mosaic tabletop—it could be either an abstract or a pictorial concept.

MATERIALS

- ready-mixed concrete and mortar patch (can be purchased at hardware stores)
- support for the mosaic: a 15- to 18-inch circle or rectangle of thin plywood can be cut, or a discarded snack table can be given a new life; large round plastic or aluminum pizza pans may be available in discount stores
- collection of various mosaic components, enough to cover each surface
- tile grout
- painting spatula or putty knife
- a pedestal for the table (could be a log or a basket or ? . . . be inventive)

PROCEDURE

1. Design your mosaics by spreading out the different stones, tiles, shards, broken pieces, glass, mica, shells, buttons, etc., on the surface to be covered.
2. Keep moving the pieces and arranging them into different configurations until a clear design starts to emerge.
3. When you have arrived at the design you want to "fix in stone," imbed your mosaic surface in mortar in sections as described next.
4. Move one small section to a board at the side, keeping the pieces in the same arrangement, so that you will be able to replace them in order.
5. Spread cement mortar on that surface segment, then carefully replace the mosaic pieces in position, setting them into the mortar.
6. Proceed to set the mosaic one small section at a time; this will help keep the arrangement.
7. Don't forget the edges of the tabletop; after the top is done, choose small pieces to fit onto the edge, and set them in place.
8. Allow the mortar to harden for the amount of time given on the container.
9. Use tile grout to fill in the spaces in the mosaic. Follow the directions and times given with the product. Excess grout should be wiped off the surface with a very squeezed-out sponge before it hardens too much.
10. When the grout has set completely, polish the new mosaic with a cloth.
11. Set the tabletop on a base, such as a base from tray tables or a cylindrical basket.

CONCLUSION

Show the students pictures of the mosaic work of Simon Rodia at Watts Towers in Los Angeles, and the mosaic walls and towers of Antoni Gaudi at the Parque Guell in Barcelona. Discuss the potentials of the student work in this technique—making something magical from bits and pieces—in relation to these modern masters. (See Figure 1–8 for an actual studio art project.)

Figure 1-8. Studio art project. Concentric mosaic design of glass tesserae, stones, shells, and broken plates. (Artwork by Susan Hogan.)

FOLLOW-UP

Compile a resource for further mosaic work. Gather pictures of mosaics ancient and modern, public and private. Continue the ongoing collection of mosaic materials for use in a larger collaborative class project.

CREATIVE WRITING

The word "mosaic" is used both literally and metaphorically to imply an artful pattern of disparate components. Discuss both meanings of the word with classmates. Then write a personal interpretation of the concept of mosaic in your own life.

TURKISH TILE ART

Seljuks were originally nomadic people from Mongolia, who settled on the fringes of the Byzantine Empire in about 1000 A.D. The city of Konya became the Seljuk sultanate in 1097, and was in its prime until the thirteenth century. The Seljuks' rich cultural life incorporated many elements from Persian civilization. Their vital and beautiful ceramic and tile art in particular had come directly from Persian influence. Seljuk tile designs show advanced color design and technical maturity. In Konya, the Seljuks built tiled mosques and *minarets* to establish centers of their Muslim faith. The interior walls, dome, and vaults of their structures were completely faced with tiles as well. The *mihrabs*, or prayer niches, inside the mosques are usually examples of extravagantly ornate tile work.

Clay tiles were cut into different geometric shapes and then glazed; stars, crosses, lozenges, octagons, and squares were combined into brilliant decorative panels. A thirteenth-century palace excavated in Konya revealed a wealth of human and animal figures painted on the tiles. Later Muslim rules forbade the use of images of living beings in art, so the decorative geometry of tilework was developed, although plant motifs were allowed.

The brilliant ceramic tiles that decorate mosques and palaces both inside and out are a striking characteristic of the architecture in Turkey today. (See Figure 1–9.) The Green Mosque in Bursa, and the Blue Mosque and Sultan Suleiman's mausoleum in Istanbul are among the many outstanding examples of tile decoration to be seen.

The city of Iznik (Biblical Nicaea) became the center of production of huge amounts of high-quality tiles for the gorgeous palaces and mosques built by the Ottoman Turks in the sixteenth century, during the reign of Sultan Suleiman the Magnificent. Iznik artisans developed a bold style in painting designs on tile. They simplified naturalistic forms of stems, leaves, flowers, and buds of different wild flowers, vines, and rosettes with great skill in quick brush drawing. Continual technical development of glaze colors was combined with more and more subtle and artful painting. Between 1530 and 1540, hyacinth, carnation, and tulip motifs (the tulip was familiar in Turkey long before it reached Holland) became the most popular designs. (See Figure 1–10.) Floral decoration became more and more elaborate and refined during the height of tile production in the sixteenth century, and *chinoiserie motifs*, unintentionally connecting the art with its remote origins in China, were frequently used.

Although there were supposedly 300 tile workshops in Iznik at the peak of royal demand at the end of the sixteenth century, ceramic production declined steeply as central Ottoman authority collapsed in the seventeenth century. Grand building projects ceased, but the enormous distribution and influence of Iznik tile art are still evident today in the brilliant architecture of that visually splendid epoch of history.

Project 1–4: Making Glazed Star Tiles

PREPARATION

Gather pictures of Turkish tiles from books and travel brochures to stimulate visual ideas for tile designs.

MATERIALS

- white low-fire clay, cone 06
- electric kiln
- paper, pencils, rulers, scissors
- fetling knife or ordinary kitchen knife
- gloss glazes in bright primary colors: red, blue, green, turquoise, black

Figure 1-10. Hatayi floral motifs from Iznik pottery are complex stylized palmettes, rosettes, or lotus blossoms. (Reprinted from *Treasury of Turkish Designs* by permission of Dover Publications.)

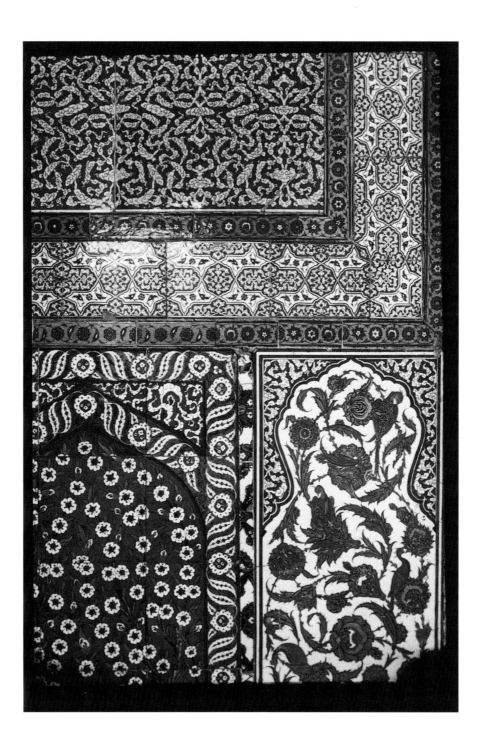

Figure 1-9. Brilliant Iznik tiles decorate walls of Ottoman mosques and palaces. (Photograph by Howard Berelson.)

PROCEDURE

1. Make a paper pattern for 8-pointed star tiles by cutting out two 4-inch squares.
2. Establish the center of each square by drawing diagonal lines from corner to corner; the point where these lines intersect is the center.
3. Place the two squares flush together, one on top of the other on another sheet of paper.
4. While holding your pencil point firmly on the center, rotate the top square so that all corners are the same size.
5. Hold the two squares firmly in this position while tracing around the star configuration.
6. Cut out the paper pattern for the 8-pointed star.
7. Wedge a lump of clay and roll it out into a flat, even slab about 1/4-inch thick.
8. Place the star pattern on the slab and cut out star shapes.
9. To prevent warping, dry these tile shapes slowly on mesh, fabric, or a paper surface, keeping them loosely covered with thin plastic, such as ordinary plastic bags.
10. Bisque fire the tiles to cone 04.
11. Adapt Turkish floral motifs (research cypress, tulip, rose, hatayi) to sketch onto the tiles with pencil.
12. As you paint your designs on the bisqued tiles with the red, green, and blue glazes, make sure you give each color area two or three coats of glaze.
13. Fire the glazed tiles to cone 06.

CONCLUSION

Display all of the star tiles together. See Figure 1–11 for an actual studio art project.

FOLLOW-UP

- Assign each student an example of Turkish Islamic architecture from the sixteenth or seventeenth century to research. Possible subjects could be the Grand Palace, the Royal Mosque, the harem in Topkapi Palace in Istanbul. Other examples can be found in guidebooks. Ask students to write a description of the structure, the tile decoration, and the history of this mosque or palace from its creation until the present day.
- Take a field trip to a tile store to see and learn about some of the contemporary applications of tile design: different materials, shapes, colors, and combinations.
- Design and make cross-shaped tiles to fit into the negative spaces between the star tiles. Then make a tile panel in which both shapes are combined.

CREATIVE WRITING

After some of your classmates have read their reports on tiled architecture aloud to the class, imagine living in one of the Sultan's palaces, and write about it.

TURKISH KILIMS

When Marco Polo traveled through Asia Minor in 1271, he observed that the most beautiful carpets in the world were made in the Seljuk cities there. The quality of these Turkish carpets was revealed to Europeans by Italian merchants, and they became very popular and desirable items. Carpets from Turkey were frequently represented in paintings by the Dutch master Holbein in the sixteenth century, and the Venetian paintings of Carpaccio show Turkish carpets covering streets and hanging from windows in the artist's depictions of festivals.

Carpets are woven with a technique of knotting the weft threads to make loops, which are then cut to form the plush pile surface. In modern Turkey, knotted carpets have traditionally been produced on large looms as an urban product for the wealthier classes and for foreign markets. (See Figure 1–12.) Kilims, in comparison, are flat-woven rugs made by rural nomadic and village women of Anatolia in their own homes for domestic use.

Figure 1-12. A young Turkish woman at work weaving a floral pattern carpet. (Photograph by Suzanne Berelson.)

Figure 1-11. Studio art project. Glazed star tiles. (Artwork by Susan Hogan.)

The cultural diversity that has thrived in Anatolia for centuries has provided a very rich matrix for its long and dynamic tradition of weaving. The interaction between peoples and ideas has contributed to a diverse and complex folklore, expressed in the flat-weaving art of each village. Techniques and designs of kilim weaving have been handed down from mother to daughter, generation after generation. Even today, as the pace of modernization, mechanization, and global communication encroaches upon the stable village cultures, distinctive styles of different villages are still identifiable.

Kilims originated as nomadic furniture, as in the cultures of Central Asia, the Middle East, and North Africa. Woven of wool from the herds of sheep and goats, kilims served as beds, couches, blankets, pillows, tables, and rugs in family tents. The woven patterns encoded symbols of the experience and beliefs of each tribe, and expressed their solidarity. The rich bright color combinations extended the warmth of home into each nomadic relocation.

Symbolic design elements traditionally woven into kilims include stylized stars to express happiness, zigzag running water motifs to express life itself, and ram's horns to express masculinity, male fertility, and heroism. *Elibelinde*, a goddess figure from Neolithic times, symbolizes both giving birth and the desire for a child. Amulets for protection from evil include scorpions and spiders, hands and fingers, and many variations of signs for the "evil eye." The tree of life, a symbol of immortality, is frequently depicted. Figures 1–13A through 1–13C show various patterns.

Until recently, kilims were woven as important dowry pieces. Marriages have always been arranged by families, and skill in weaving has been a desirable characteristic of a prospective bride. A young woman's artistic ability and industry in creating a wealth of beautiful, useful, and valuable kilims for the family home—for comfort, for prestige, and to offer in exchange for other essential goods—has been an essential role in community life. In the villages, kilims have been used as rugs, curtains, prayer rugs, animal trappings, and made into bags for storage and transportation. They are given to the mosque for prayer, and for hangings to separate the men from the women.

Rapid changes in contemporary life are affecting these customs of Turkish life. Commercialization and economic pressure have caused a loss of craft and identity as families prefer to educate their young women for more economically rewarding jobs in modern society. Where the motivation for weaving kilims has changed from personal expression to monetary gain, a corresponding decline in quality is usually evident. Turkish kilims, because of their elaborate and satisfying patterns in brilliant and varied color combinations, are in great demand by tourists and by the home decorating market in the more industrialized countries of the West, where many rug stores and furniture stores feature a dazzling array of kilim examples. They are also made into pillows, furniture, bags, and slippers for export. (See Figure 1–14.)

Project 1–5: Making Colored Drawings of Kilims on Cloth

Kilim patterns provide a wonderfully stimulating range of visual information that can be explored with crayons, markers, and colored pencils.

PREPARATION

Find color reproductions of kilims in books and magazines, or have students visit a rug store to take photographs of kilims for their design resource. Some art galleries may feature kilims.

Figure 1-14. Chairs upholstered with handwoven Turkish kilims are imported by the Istanbul Grand Bazaar in New York City. (Courtesy of H̃useyin Aktuğ.)

MATERIALS

- rectangles of white or pale-colored cloth, approximately 6" × 9" (use canvas, denim, or muslin—(sources can be recycled garments brought by the students, or tablecloths and curtains from the thrift store, etc.)
- pencils, rulers
- colored pencils, crayons, markers

Figures 1-13A, 1-13B, and 1-13C. Kilims imported from Turkey displayed at the Istanbul Grand Bazaar in New York City. (Courtesy of Ḥuseyin Aktuğ.)

PROCEDURE

1. Selecting from your design research, sketch kilim designs onto cloth.
2. You will gradually arrive at a pattern to develop into a finished drawing with the colored pencils or markers.

CONCLUSION

Make an accordion-fold "book" of card paper with pages large enough to mount student kilim drawings on each page. Mount each drawing with the student's written description of the kilim adjacent to it. This arrangement will make an attractive tabletop display.

FOLLOW-UP

Take a field trip to a rug store or the rug department in a furniture store to extend the students' awareness of the vitality and beauty of rug and carpet designs from various countries in the world. They could take photographs of the rugs for a design resource file, collect brochures, or interview the merchants about how imported rugs are manufactured and sold.

CREATIVE WRITING

How are rugs made with modern-day technology? Compare this process with how rural and village women have made kilims in their own homes.

Project 1–6: Collage of Hotel Room Decorated with Kilims

Many luxurious hotels have been constructed recently at Turkey's numerous beautiful tourist attractions. (See Figure 1–15.) Imagining a vacation at one of these places could become a concrete visualization of a visit to Turkey.

Figure 1-15. This distinctive hotel in Cappadocia is one of many world-class accommodations recently developed during Turkey's tourist boom. (Photograph by Howard Berelson.)

After students construct the interior design of a new hotel room by collaging pictures of furniture cut from magazines and catalogs, they can decorate their room in Turkish style by adding color drawings of kilims on the couch, bed, floor, walls, and chairs. Markers, crayons, and colored pencils are vivid and easy to work with on cloth, which adds tactile elements to the collage.

PREPARATION

Collect a pile of home decorating magazines and catalogs for pictures of furniture and room interiors. Pictures of new Turkish hotels can be obtained in brochures from tour companies.

MATERIALS

- home furnishings advertisments
- paper, pencils, scissors, glue sticks, white glue, ruler
- cloth, recycled, from previous project
- colored pencils, markers, and/or crayons

PROCEDURE

1. Cut out furniture from home furnishings circulars, advertisements, and magazines.
2. As you arrange your assortment of furniture on the page to develop a room collage, positions of the walls and floor will become apparent, and lines can be drawn with the ruler to indicate them.
3. Add windows looking out onto the Turkish landscape with sections of scenery cut from the brochures.
4. Before pasting the furniture in place, use the pictures as patterns to cut out pieces of the cloth for kilims to cover the bed, the couches, and the floor.
5. Glue furniture in place with a glue stick.
6. Refer to picture books of kilims to draw kilim patterns in color on the cut pieces of cloth representing the rug, the covers for the bed, couches, chairs and pillows, or hanging on the walls.
7. Glue kilims in place with white glue. If necessary, press the collages flat by placing them under a weighted board until dry.

CONCLUSION

Combine all of the students' room collages into one large collage (like a dollhouse) to construct a fanciful resort hotel interior. Figure 1–16 shows an actual studio art project.

FOLLOW-UP

Have students select a particular place to locate their resort hotel by researching possible locations in picture books and guidebooks of Turkey. They can explain the appeal of its geography, history, archaeology, and culture for international tourists and students in writing a promotional brochure.

CREATIVE WRITING

Remember the fairy tale about the magic carpet? Imagine flying over Asia Minor on a magic carpet and describe the sights and sensations as you cruise by on the carpet.

Figure 1-16. Studio art project. Colored pencil drawings of typical Turkish kilims add plush comfort to this interior design collage. (Artwork by Susan Hogan.)

Vocabulary Worksheet for Turkey

Look up the following vocabulary words in a dictionary, write the definition, and then use the word in writing a sentence about Turkey. Use a separate sheet of paper for this activity.

Aegean	iconoclasts
agora	infrastructure
amphitheater	kilim
antiquity	looms
archaeology	Magna Graecia
Asia Minor	matrix
basilica	metropolis
Bosporus	mihrab
Byzantine	minarets
chinoiserie	mosaic
Dardanelles	mosque
dowry	Seljuk
eccentric	solidarity
Elibelinde	straits
epoch	subtle
excavations	tesserae
fervor	turquoise
flat-woven	zealously

Name _____ Date _____

Geography Worksheet for Turkey

Find the answers to these problems in world atlases and encyclopedias. Use the back of this sheet if you need more space.

- What geographical attractions contribute to Turkey's appeal to international tourism?

  _____

  _____

- Examine the Aegean coast of Turkey and list all of the Greek Islands that look close enough to be within sight of it.

  _____

  _____

- What countries of the Middle East border Turkey?

  _____

  _____

- Locate the Kurdish areas near the border of Turkey and Iraq. Why do you think the Kurds would want to become a separate nation?

  _____

  _____

- Locate the Russian ports on the Black Sea from which oil tankers begin their journey to the Bosporus, and describe the water route these Russian ships take between their Black Sea ports of origin and the Atlantic Ocean.

  _____

  _____

- Identify the largest lake in Turkey, describe its location, and list some of its distinguishing features.

  _____

  _____

Geography Worksheet for Turkey (continued)

- Describe the path of the Euphrates River from its source in Turkey to the Persian Gulf. Do the same for the Tigris River. Why are these two rivers so famous?

  _____

  _____

- Find the location of Mt. Ararat in Eastern Turkey, and describe its significance in the Old Testament of the Bible.

  _____

  _____

- What are the major food crops of central and southern Turkey? What crops are produced mainly for export to other countries?

  _____

  _____

- Identify the Turkish towns and cities on the Black Sea, and list their population sizes and economic resources.

  _____

  _____

Related Assignments for Turkey

1. **Follow the news.** Current Turkish issues that are regularly in the news include the difficulty of the Prime Minister balancing foreign relations with Arab nations and with the West, and the effort of the Turkish Kurds to become a separate nation.

2. **Biography**
   - Ataturk
   - Sultan Suleiman the Magnificent
   - Constantine the Great
   - St. Paul
   - Emperor Justinian and Empress Theodora
   - Homer

3. **History of empires**
   - Persian Empire
   - Alexander's Empire
   - Roman Empire
   - Byzantine Empire
   - Ottoman Empire

4. **Economics.** Research the economic impact of tourism and international trade on the national economy of Turkey.

5. **Biblical History.** Identify Biblical locations in Turkey.

6. **Archaeology.**
   - Research the Roman cities of Asia Minor (Pergamum, Ephesus, Smyrna) and Antioch, city of the New Testament.
   - Find the story of the archaeology of Troy and Heinrich Schliemann.

7. **Art Appreciation**
   - Study Turkish miniature paintings.
   - Locate Turkish carpets in European Renaissance paintings by Hans Holbein and by Carpaccio.

8. **Geology.** Research the formation of the tufa landscape of Cappodocia, and the way that humans have adapted this natural rock terrain for habitation.

RESOURCES FOR TEACHING

BOOKS

Akar, Azade. *Treasury of Turkish Designs, 670 Motifs from Iznik Pottery*. New York: Dover Publications, 1988.

al Fārūqī, Ismail R. and Lois Lamya al Fārūqī. *The Cultural Atlas of Islam*. New York: Macmillan, 1986.

Demirsar, Metin (ed.). *Turkish Coast, Insight Guides*. Boston: Houghton Mifflin, 1996.

Eames, Andrew (ed.). *Turkey, Insight Guides*. Boston: Houghton Mifflin, 1995.

Frank, Harry Thomas (ed.). *Atlas of the Bible Lands*. Maplewood, NJ: Hammond, Inc., 1984.

Hull, Alastair and Jose Luczyc-Wyhowska. *Kilim, The Complete Guide*. London: Chronicle Books, Thames & Hudson, 1993.

Vance, Peggy and Celia Goodrick-Clarke. *Mosaic Book, Ideas, Projects and Techniques*. North Pomfret, VT: Trafalgar Square Publishing, 1995.

PERIODICALS

Archaeology, published by-monthly by the Archaeological Institute of America, 135 William Street, New York, NY 10030

Washington Report on Middle East Affairs, published eight times yearly at 1902 18th St., Washington, D.C. 20009-1707. Phone: (202) 939-6050.

NATIONAL TOURIST OFFICE

Turkish Information Office
821 United Nations Plaza
New York, NY 10017
(212) 687-2194/5/6

TOURIST BROCHURES

Pacha Tours
1560 Broadway, Suite 316
New York, NY 10036
(212) 764-4080; (800) 722-4288

BIBLIOGRAPHY

Akar, Azade. *Treasury of Turkish Designs, 670 Motifs from Iznik Pottery*. New York: Dover Publications, 1988.

Blair, Sheila S. and Jonathan M. Bloom. *The Art and Architecture of Islam 1250-1800*. New York: Penguin Books, 1987.

Byzantium. City of Gold, City of Faith. London: Orbis Publishing, 1983.

Darke, Diana. *Guide to Aegean and Mediterranean Turkey*. London: Michael Haag Ltd., 1989.

Darke, Diana. *Discovery Guide to Eastern Turkey*. London: Michael Haag Ltd., 1990

Linde, Helmut. *Baedecker's Istanbul*. New York and Canada: Prentice Hall Press, 1987.

Lord Kinross. *Hagia Sophia*. New York: Newsweek, 1972.

Petsopoulos, Yanni (ed.). *Tulips, Arabesques, & Turbans. Decorative Arts from the Ottoman Empire*. New York: Abbeville Press, 1982.

Riley, Noel. *Tile Art*. Secaucus, New Jersey: Chartwell, 1987.

Talbot Rice, David. *Art of the Byzantine Era*. London: Thames & Hudson, 1963.

SECTION TWO
Ireland

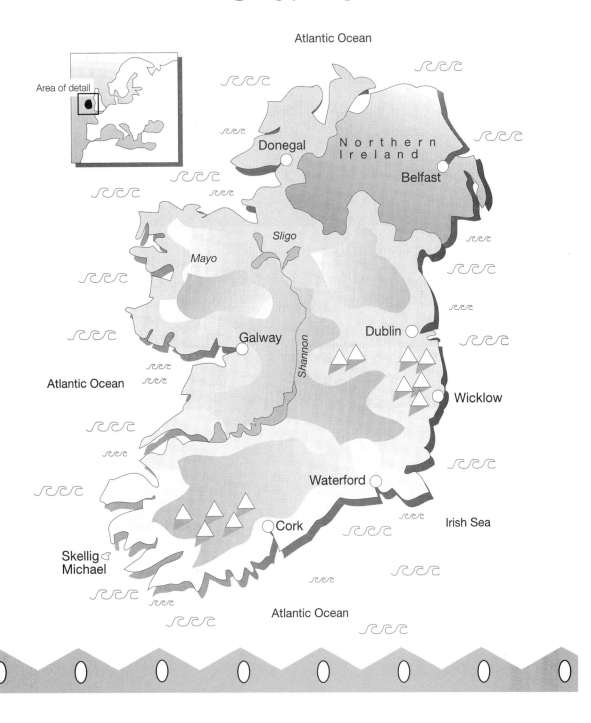

Atlantic Ocean

Area of detail

Donegal

Northern Ireland

Belfast

Sligo

Mayo

Galway

Shannon

Dublin

Wicklow

Atlantic Ocean

Waterford

Irish Sea

Cork

Skellig Michael

Atlantic Ocean

A BRIEF HISTORY OF IRELAND

From Ireland, millions of people have emigrated throughout the years to destinations all over the world. The population of Ireland today is about 5 million people, but there are at least 70 million Irish people in the rest of the world. Many of them left their country to escape the misfortunes of Irish history—pressures of war, famine, oppression, injustice, and overpopulation forced them to seek opportunities to build new lives in exile. They settled in Australia and New Zealand, South America, the continent of Europe, Canada, and the United States. The Irish potato famine of 1845–1847, when a million people starved to death because the potato crop had failed, was a disaster that caused many of those who survived to flee to more prosperous countries, and especially to the United States.

At least ten of the American men who signed the Declaration of Independence in 1776 had originally come to this country from Ireland, and no fewer than ten U.S. presidents have had Irish ancestors. In recent years, Irish emigrants searching for their family roots are among the millions of tourists who travel to the Emerald Isle (See Figure 2–1.) every year.

Figure 2-1. Map of Ireland. This is a simplified locator map for quick reference. Students can look up a more detailed map of Ireland in a world atlas.

The Irish people have a reputation for friendliness, and are welcoming to visitors. Bed-and-breakfast accommodations in private homes are found in every village and town, and many of the old castles have been transformed into spectacular hotels. The vividly green terrain, produced by the very high humidity, has been shaped into world-class golf courses in many areas. The green green grass, growing in limestone soil, has provided a calcium-rich diet for raising strong and healthy race horses. Horse racing is also a popular vacation attraction.

The beautiful green landscape of Eire, the westernmost country in Europe, has played a major role in the work of its world-famous poets, writers, and playwrights. (See Figure 2–2.) J. M. Synge wrote the dramas *Riders to the Sea* and *The Playboy of the Western World* about life in the Aran Islands. George Russell (whose penname was AE) was a poet, painter, and mystic who regularly returned to the wild and lonely country of Donegal, where he felt he could connect with "memories from the beginning of the world." George Moore's writing was inspired by his life of leisure on the 12,000 family acres in rural Mayo. James Joyce and Samuel Beckett, who are both considered among the greatest writers of the twentieth century, left Ireland as young men, and produced their great works in exile from their homeland.

Figure 2-2. The Ring of Kerry, a panoramic route around the Iveragh peninsula in southwest Ireland.

W. B. Yeats won the Nobel Prize for literature in 1923. Much of his poetry celebrates the beauty and mystery of the natural surroundings of Sligo on the Atlantic Coast, where he spent many boyhood summers at the home of his mother's parents, aunts, and uncles. Sligo was the land of Yeats's eternal youth, which he visited again and again in his poetry. His very well-known poem, "The Lake Isle of Innisfree," evokes an idyllic life close to nature. The poet's brother was Jack Yeats, one of Ireland's foremost painters, whose paintings now sell for over a million dollars whenever they appear at auction. Their father was a portrait painter who predicted that his sons would far surpass his own modest reputation.

We can begin to get to know this land by appreciating its natural, distinctive scenic identity, as the great Irish writers and artists have always done. The long rugged coastline where the Atlantic Ocean meets dramatic cliffs and rocks and the natural, unspoiled mountain areas are beautiful scenic attractions. The atmosphere changes all day long, because southwest winds blowing across the Gulf Stream in the Atlantic Ocean bring constant changes in weather. As wet clouds are continually blown across the land, the daylight keeps changing from sunny to cloudy to rainy and back again. The landscape colors are rich and varied, remaining in the cool range: hundreds of foliage greens, watery blues, and the violets of distance, sky, and atmosphere.

If you were to take a painting trip through Ireland, you would see infinite possibilities for subject matter. Green fields are divided into brilliant patchwork by lines of rocks defining characteristic patterns. Many lakes and rivers saturate the landscape. Another unique feature of the Irish terrain is the extensive peat bogs, formed of accumulated dead plants in water-logged basins. Blocks of peat are mined by hand, dried, and stacked for use as fuel for cooking and heating.

As a traveller moves through the landscape, his or her point of view keeps changing, and new combinations of landscape subject matter present themselves at every point. Since you probably won't be accompanying your class on a field trip to Ireland in the near future, photographs of Irish scenes can substitute for first-hand experience. Many beautiful picture books are available in libraries, and in travel brochures and postcards. Painting from photographs is a great way to explore exotic landscapes while working on techniques of water-color painting. The skill and confidence gained by making small watercolor studies can then be applied to visual studies of architectural styles, of stained-glass designs, and of the symbols of blazonry. The best of these small paintings can be combined with the best descriptive writing and compiled into a book to be bound with the embossed brass book cover, as described in Project 2–3.

Project 2–1: Painting Irish Landscape from Photographs

Pictorial composition, structure, and color are given by the photographer, leaving the student free to explore other issues of painting technique. Three different approaches are suggested here, and many other assignments with watercolor could be developed.

PREPARATION

Have students do picture research in the local library, at the travel agency, or approach the Irish Tourist Board for visual information. Picture postcards are an available resource for studying the specific qualities of this particular land. Have each student select three or four favorite pictures to work with.

MATERIALS

- watercolor paints: box of assorted colors
- brushes
- 6" × 9" sheets of all-purpose paper
- pencils
- water and containers

PROCEDURE

1. Analyze the division of pictorial space into foreground, middle ground, and background as students sketch these three areas on their paper.

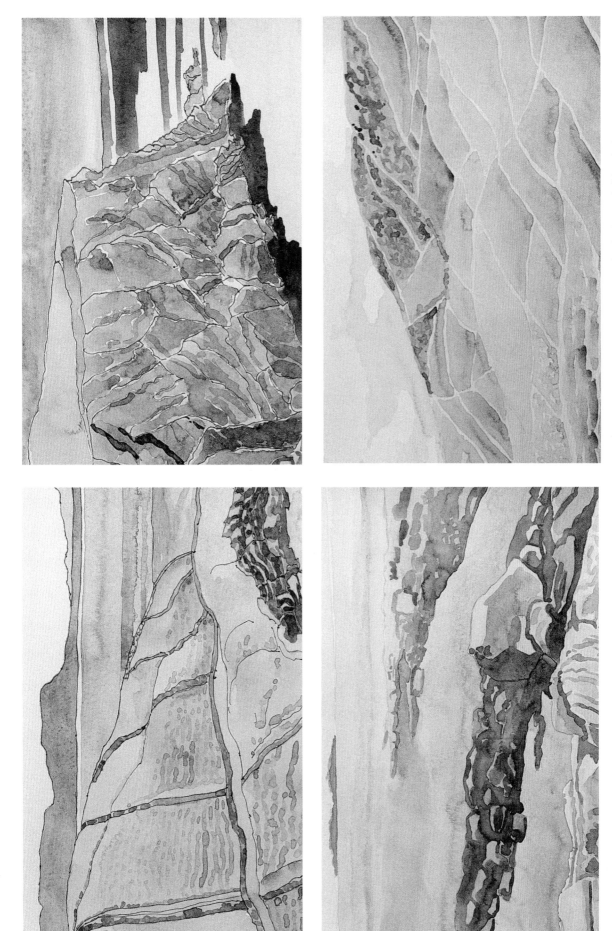

Figures 2-3A, 2-3B, 2-3C, and 2-3D. Studio art project. Watercolors of Irish landscape painted on location by Marjorie Shaw Kubach depict fields of characteristic green patchwork, the dramatic rocky coast, and moisture-laden sky.

2. Develop this space with two different *value gradations*. Use a neutral gray, and work from a light foreground to a dark background.

3. Paint a second version from dark foreground to light background.

4. Play with the sky tone in relation to the value range of landscape shapes: try a dark sky, a very light sky, a middle-range sky.

5. Explore variations in *color intensity* in the same manner. Paint a pale foreground to a more intense background.

6. In the next painting, set up an intense foreground fading gradually into a pale background.

7. Build up color intensity with washes of more paint. Gradually strengthen and emphasize the color harmonies.

8. Experiment with *changes in focus* by painting one select area in sharp focus, using softer more blended painting in the surrounding areas.

CONCLUSION

Put all of these student painting exercises up on one wall and have the students look silently at all of them together. Point out particular color harmonies, atmosphere, and pictorial movements that are evident in the paintings, and encourage students to verbalize constructive criticism. This dialogue develops the students' vocabulary for discussing visual work. After your verbal discussion, have students write brief descriptions of their pictures. See Figures 2–3A through 2–3D for actual studio art projects.

FOLLOW-UP

Students can create a travelogue for one small area of Ireland by combining a series of small watercolor paintings with a written description of the place. This class project can be displayed and then become part of the material for a book of paintings and designs from Irish culture, concurrently with doing the embossed metal book cover project.

CREATIVE WRITING

Create written descriptions of the landscape subject matter, as described in the Conclusion.

IRISH STONE STRUCTURES

Another distinctive feature of the Irish landscape is the vast amount of ruined churches, abbeys, monasteries, and round towers, as well as stone circles and dolmens from the pre-Christian era. Ruins of the past are encountered everywhere, stone reminders of the common historic experience of this people.

- **Stone dolmens**, or megaliths, were left by the earliest known inhabitants of Ireland, more than 3,000 years ago. Pre-Celtic peoples marked their sites of worship and of graves with massive standing stones and "tables" constructed of huge rocks.

- **Hill of Tara** is the heart of Celtic Ireland. It was the seat of power of the High Kings, who were crowned on a stone called the Coronation Stone.

- **Beehive cells** (clochain) are rounded huts of drystone masonry, more than 1,000 years old, still to be seen on the island of Great Skellig, where Saint Finan is said to have established one of the very first Christian monasteries in Ireland. The stone huts were used by monks for solitary contemplation.

- **Round towers** are a distinctively Irish structure, built between 900 and about 1200 A.D. There are about 70 still standing at sites of destroyed monasteries. They functioned as bell towers, lookouts, storage rooms, and retreats. The entrances are many feet above ground; monks used a ladder to enter, then pulled it up after themselves when they took refuge from marauding Vikings or from Irish warlords.

- **Irish-Romanesque churches** were built in the twelfth century, slightly later than the Romanesque style in the rest of Europe. Cormac's Chapel, at Cashel, is a unique example of this style.

- **Abbeys**, now in ruins, were the huge monastic establishments, religious cities of the Gothic era.

- **Castles** of stone were built by the conquering Normans in the thirteenth century to replace their earlier *motte and bailey* fortifications. A rectangular plan of curtain walls, cylindrical defense towers at the corners, surrounded by a moat was the edifice to enforce their dominance. Castles became the nuclei of towns and the basis of political and economic power. (See Figures 2–4A and 2–4B.)

Figure 2-4A. Ruins of Donegal Castle. (Photograph by Marjorie Shaw Kubach.)

Figure 2-4B. Ruins of Delvin Castle. (Photograph by Marjorie Shaw Kubach.)

- **Traditional houses** of a single story, a thatched roof, and a rectangular plan have been built with the same characteristic size and shape from neolithic times until the present.

- **Georgian style** refers to the neoclassical architecture of the eighteenth century, during the reigns of the English King Georges. Many villas were built for the English nobles who occupied Irish land. Abundant plaster relief decoration on walls and ceilings, or stuccowork, was very popular.

- **Neo-Gothic** was the result of the surge of reconstructions and new buildings in the nineteenth century, when architects drew inspiration from the Gothic era. Many neo-Gothic churches still dominate the landscape of towns and cities today, reminders of the centuries-old conflict between Catholics and Protestants.

Project 2–2: Making a Stone Collage Castle

PREPARATION

Collecting flat stones that could be used for a picture mosaic should be an ongoing task well before undertaking this project, to insure that the class has an ample supply of material. Using stones as raw material is intended to direct the students' attention to the geological origin of all kinds of human habitats.

Assign a different castle to each student. Have them research it in history books and guide books to Ireland, as well as tourist brochures. A few of the most interesting and picturesque are: Castle Coole, Limerick Castle, Donegal, and Malahide Castle. Students will need to find a visual image of the castle, and write a brief history.

Before the students start to make their stone picture, have them do one or two studies of their particular subject in watercolor, to become familiar with the dimensions and proportions, planes, and shading of the architecture.

MATERIALS

- plenty of flat stones of different colors and shapes (large stones can be broken up with a hammer on pavement or cement, or on a brick in the classroom)
- tile cement or white glue
- cardboard (cut off the sides of corrugated boxes, leaving 2-inch angles attached at the corners so the wall can be made to stand up)
- spray sealer for cardboard to keep it from warping badly
- shellac or clear acrylic medium for a final coat on the stones

PROCEDURE

1. Referring to your picture reference, begin to arrange stones on the cardboard surface in a free interpretation of the castle wall.
2. Develop the flat stone picture by using the different types and colors of stone to show gates, windows, towers, turrets, etc., in some detail. The top of the support can be cut into a silhouette of turrets and towers for extra appeal.
3. When the picture is complete, adhere the stones section by section. Move one area of stones to the side, apply glue to the cardboard surface, then press the stones into the adhesive in their previous arrangement.
4. Seal the stone picture with a coat of shellac or clear acrylic medium.

CONCLUSION

The castles should be able to stand up if sides of the box have been left attached. Display them with labels of the student's description of the history and traditions of each place. See Figure 2–5 for an actual studio art project of a stone collage castle.

FOLLOW-UP

Interior studies of castle life can be made with paint and colored pencil on cardboard cut in the same format, then displayed standing behind the stone wall.

Figure 2-5. Studio art project. The castle wall of different stone textures is adhered to corrugated cardboard. (Artwork by Susan Hogan.)

CREATIVE WRITING

As an inhabitant of this historic castle, how would you describe your life to a visitor from the late twentieth century?

IRISH ARTISTRY IN METAL

The Celtic peoples came to Ireland from further east, from England, Wales, and the Continent, about 600 B.C. They established settlements of warlike family groups, who were always fighting with each other to retain their territory. In the first centuries of the Christian era, these Celts regularly raided the coast of Roman Britain, across the Irish Sea, to capture slaves.

Saint Patrick, the legendary saint of Ireland, was first taken to Ireland as a slave snatched from his family home in Britain. He was forced to serve as a shepherd—alone, naked, and hungry—for three years, so miserable that he began to pray constantly. In a dream, he had a vision that his ship was waiting, so he walked through the wilderness to the coast, boarded the ship leaving the country, and eventually made his way back to his family in England. No longer at home there, Patrick went to the south of France to attend a seminary for the

Catholic priesthood. In the year 432 A.D., at the age of 48, he returned to Ireland as a Christian missionary.

Saint Patrick set about converting the pagan Celtic people to Christianity. He established monastic communities, where illiterate monks gathered and learned to read and write. As the rest of Europe floundered in the darkness of barbarian takeover at the fall of the Roman Empire, the monks of Ireland, protected by their isolated location at the western edge of Europe, preserved the learning of the Greek and Roman traditions. The monastic scribes made beautifully illuminated copies of the precious manuscripts of European Christianity: the gospels and the writings of Christian saints.

Christianity provided new outlets for the decorative tradition of Celtic art, a highly developed metal artistry that was intricate, brilliant, and exquisitely wrought. The rich mineral deposits in Ireland had been mined in the Bronze Age, about 1700 B.C. The abundant gold nuggets in the rivers of County Wicklow and gold from the ancient mine under the peat bogs in west Cork were hammered into thin sheets; then raised designs of circles were hammered into these gold sheets from the back. In the third century B.C. (Iron Age), new emblems in metalwork appeared: spirals and stylized plant, animal, and bird forms. (See Figure 2–7.)

In the many monasteries, chalices, bells, and shrines were crafted to contain objects of veneration. Fine filigree work in gold and silver—ornamented with inset gems, glass, and amber—reached a stylistic peak from the seventh to ninth centuries. (See Figure 2-6.) Irish monks who traveled to the continent as missionaries took samples of this unique artwork with them. Vikings raided Irish monasteries, stealing the gorgeous metalwork to take back to Norway. Eventually the Vikings established the secular trading ports of Dublin, Cork, and Limerick, opening up markets for metal art. When the Normans invaded in 1169, the relentless Anglo oppression did its best to eliminate this native Irish art.

Project 2–3: Making an Embossed Brass Book Cover

PREPARATION

Study photographs of this early metal art for inspiration. Refer to books of Celtic design. Sketch different motifs and combine the ones you like to develop a 6" × 8" rectangular layout. Figure 2–7 shows Celtic motifs.

MATERIALS

- paper, pencil, and ruler
- 36-gauge brass tooling foil (can be ordered from school art supply catalogs)
- scissors
- X-acto™ knife
- modeling tools (wood or plastic chopsticks, wooden skewers, plastic spoons and knives, ballpoint pens, dental tools, icepicks, screwdrivers)
- quartz pebbles, glass gems, marbles to use as "gems"
- silicone glue
- cardboard for backing
- transparent tape or masking tape
- soft cloth

Figure 2-6. Bronze and silver book shrine Soiscél Molaise, Devenish. (Courtesy of National Museum of Ireland, Dublin.)

Figure 2-7. Celtic motifs of interlacing knots. (Reprinted by permission of Dover Publications.)

Figure 2-7. (Continued)

PROCEDURE

1. **Important!** Handle sharp edges with great care—this metal foil can cut seriously! Protect edges by temporarily binding them with transparent tape or masking tape.

2. Explore the material. Take a scrap for experimentation and try different tools and different pressures to make marks. Learn how marking on one side will create raised marks on the reverse, and use this knowledge in designing a book cover.

3. Use paper, pencil, and ruler to lay out the design. Divide the surface into squares or rectangles, use circles within squares, detail with interlacing designs. Plan the placement of gems.

4. Place the design over the brass, hold it firmly in place, and transfer by pressing gently with a ballpoint pen or similar tool.

5. Embossing is raised gradually. Push out the larger areas first, developing form in the flat metal by turning it back and forth, working first on one side, then on the other.

6. Develop smaller detail areas with a pointed tool.

7. Cut a rectangle out of cardboard (a piece of corrugated box is good) to fit the finished piece. Fold four edge flaps over this backing.

8. Set "gems" into the completed surface with a dab of clear silicone glue.

9. Polish the surface with a soft cloth.

10. If desired, antique the surface by applying a thin wash of stain made with diluted paint.

CONCLUSION

The completion of this gorgeous cover should be an inspiration to continue making high-quality special art. Figure 2–8 shows an actual studio art project.

Figure 2-8. Studio art project. Embossed brass book cover with gems of pebbles and glass. (Artwork by Susan Hogan.)

FOLLOW-UP

Students can make watercolor studies of other metal work designs to include in their books.

CREATIVE WRITING

Write descriptions of selected Irish metal art to augment the visual material for your book.

STAINED GLASS IN IRELAND

The Gothic cathedrals built by Irish Christians during the great European age of cathedral building, during the twelfth and thirteenth centuries, were mostly destroyed during centuries of armed conflict and turbulence. The stone traceries, or window frameworks, are sometimes still standing in the ruins of these old cathedrals, but whatever original glass had been in the windows has been gone for centuries. (See Figure 2–9.) We can assume that the windows were created in Gothic style, as in most English, French, and German cathedrals—conceived as narrative, telling and retelling the familiar Bible stories in images of brilliant translucent glass, constructed by the glass artisans attached to each monastery.

In the nineteenth century, after the Catholic Emancipation, there was a resurgence of church construction in the neo-Gothic style and a great demand for stained glass. The Irish revival in stained-glass art was centered in the An Tur Gloine (the Tower of Glass), a workshop founded by Sarah Purser, and managed by A. E. Child. Trained in the William Morris studio, center of the Arts & Crafts movement in England, Child had been invited to Dublin in 1903 to teach the craft of stained glass to a group of Irish painters.

Harry Clarke was one of the outstanding stained-glass artists in this resurgence of inspiration from historic Celtic heritage, a Celtic Revival in all of the arts. Working from his studio in Dublin, Clarke developed an international reputation, gaining prizes and commissions worldwide. Examples of his prolific glass artistry can be seen in St. Patrick's Purgatory on Station Island in Donegal, in St. Mel's at Longford, and in Dublin at St. Joseph Ternure. Eleven exemplary windows by Clarke in Honan Collegiate Chapel in Cork, along with eight windows by members of An Tur Gloine and the furnishings and other decorations, are beautiful examples of the Celtic Revival style. The brilliant St. Patrick window from this series, illustrated in Figure 2–10 conveys a universal sense of harmony in the saturated hues of purple, green, yellow, blue, and red, set off by the strong black outlines.

On the west coast just south of Galway, St. Brendan's cathedral in Loughrea contains a treasury of artworks by many Celtic Revival artisans, including a series of beautiful windows by Michael Healy. The cathedral honors Saint Brendan, one of Ireland's most beloved saints, who set sail from West of Ireland in the year 900 into the unknown Atlantic on a sea voyage that lasted for nine years, reputedly carrying him to the wild shores of the New World and back again. Saint Brendan's journey belongs to the Irish tradition of intrepid saints who extended their influence, curiosity, and learning far into the surrounding world.

Project 2–4: Painting on Glass (or Plexiglas™)

Stained-glass windows are traditionally constructed by cutting out shapes of flat colored glass and binding them together into units with flexible lead caming. Painting on these windows with enamels and stains was a part of the craft, to develop detail and refinement in rendering

Figure 2-9. Stone tracery once framed glass windows in a Gothic cathedral. (Photograph by Marjorie Shaw Kubach.)

Figure 2-10. Stained glass window of St. Patrick from a series of eleven in Celtic Revival style by Harry Clarke. Permission for reproduction from Board Governors, Honan Hostel, University College, Cork.

and subtlety in tone. For this project, we will set aside the intricate craft skill of stained-glass work, and explore painting directly on glass.

Study photos of stained-glass windows to analyze the principles of design in combining segments of saturated translucent color with traceries of black lines. Students could choose a few of which to make watercolor studies.

Pictures or photographs placed under a clear windowpane can be directly translated into stained-glass style painting. Try developing a portrait in Gothic style from photos of family or friends.

PREPARATION

Have students search for pictures of the bold and simplified glass windows of the Celtic Revival in travel brochures and art books. They can bring in color photographs of family or friends to use in painting a portrait in stained-glass style.

MATERIALS

- pane of window glass (*Note*: If using glass is not advisable in your classroom situation, use Plexiglas™ as a support for the translucent paintings.)
- sketches/studies of other windows
- black tape for edges
- photos of friends and family
- oil paints
- a solvent (turpentine or Turpenoid)
- a palette for mixing colors
- brushes
- containers
- pencils

PROCEDURE

1. If your glass isn't framed, **bind edges of glass with tape**.
2. Place portrait photo under the glass.
3. Use thin markers to draw the design onto the glass. The lines can be easily wiped off and revised.
4. Select a limited palette of colors for your color scheme.
5. Color each separate block with a thin glaze of oil paint thinned with turpentine.
6. As colors dry, they can be deepened by adding more layers of thin paint.
7. Painting the face: Over the area of dry flesh-tone paint, delineate the face in detail with pencil, closely following the photograph placed under the glass. Then add subtle shadows and highlights with thinned paint.
8. Paint thick black lines between the segments of pure color.
9. Optional: Varnish with clear gloss.

CONCLUSION

How can these new paintings on glass be displayed so light shines through them? (See Figure 2–11 for an actual studio art project.)

FOLLOW-UP

- Take a field trip to a local church to see actual stained-glass art as it is integrated into architectural space to create light and atmosphere.
- Do further research on stained glass in the Gothic era and in the neo-Gothic era in Europe. Study techniques of stained glass used through the centuries.

CREATIVE WRITING

Write a descriptive magazine article about this group of paintings on glass, developing authentic personal adjectives for color and light.

HERALDRY IN IRELAND

Heraldry was brought to Ireland by the Norman invasion in 1169. During the previous century—just after the Norman invasion of England in 1066—full metal armor and helmets had developed to completely cover the faces of warriors and their leaders. The need to identify friend or foe in battle led to the use of simple, bold, unmistakeable visual symbols on shields, banners, and coats-of-arms (cloth tunics worn over steel armor). This colorful blazonry in all materials dramatized the military pomp and splendor of battle and tournament for the centuries up until the introduction of firearms in about 1376.

The basis of heraldic insignia is a shield, the instrument of defense, and the ideal field on which to display identifying signs. The visual language of blazonry developed a very specific vocabulary throughout the centuries, even though immediate practical need for it passed with the end of the Gothic era. The *field* is the surface of the shield, or background. Each specific emblem, or image placed within the field, is known as a *charge*. Basic divisions of the field are described as chief, fess, base, pale, bend, and quarter. The *crest* is the helmet or crown above the shield; the *mantle* is the stylized drapery around it, protecting the metal from the full heat of the sun.

In Ireland, heraldry was absorbed as a system of family identification and connection with history. The Irish had totally different traditions of battle and warfare, and never adopted customs of military pomp and pageantry from the rest of Europe. Whereas English blazonry had become grandiose in its expression of competition, rank, and status, the simpler and more democratic Irish clung to signs of their past. In Irish heraldry can be found combinations of Gaelic, Norman, and Anglo emblems. Unique ancient Gaelic charges are the stag, the boar, the salmon, and an open right hand. The oak tree is a symbolic connection with the ancient Druidic religion. These heraldic insignia are instantly readable history, identifying association of family with place and name. They are threads tying present experience to family roots and layers of time, connecting identity through hundreds of years of turbulence and upheaval.

Today in any city or town in Ireland, heraldic emblems or coats of arms can be seen as architectural ornamentation in all materials: as stonecarving in gates, doorways, walls and

Figure 2-11. Studio art project. Painting of a family portrait on glass. (Artwork by Susan Hogan.)

tombs, woodcarving in mantels and panelling, metalwork in brass and bronze, medallions of glass in windows, and embroidered or painted as banners. (See Figure 2–12.) There is a museum devoted to heraldry in Dublin that includes not only traditional family insignia, but signs and seals of nations, universities, and ecclesiastical orders. The national insignia of Ireland is a golden harp upon a blue shield, and the city of Dublin is signified by three castles set on a plain field.

Figure 2-12. Heraldic emblem; stone carvings of family insignia set into walls and gates to identify the inhabitants. (Courtesy of Irish Tourist Board.)

Project 2–5: Carving a Heraldic Emblem in Clay

Almost any object can be used in blazonry. Students can invent a new combination of symbols for personal expression. Refer to books on heraldry for the categories of *charges*: animals, birds, insects, flowers, trees, stars, planets, and so on, stimulating the students to select and develop their own emblems. Figure 2–13 shows a variety of heraldic designs.

PREPARATION

The basic elements of blazonry, or heraldic design, are readily available in reference books. Boldness, clarity, and simplicity are qualities of classic coats of arms. Combining the essential

Figure 2-13. A page of heraldic designs. (Reprinted by permission of Dover Publications.)

components of shield, crest, mantle, and two or three charges, students can put together their own unique personal emblem.

MATERIALS

- modeling tools
- white clay, cone 06
- 6-inch unwaxed paper plate
- plastic bag for slow drying
- electric kiln
- neutral color underglaze or stain

PROCEDURE

1. Wedge a lump of clay.
2. Press clay into the paper plate; smooth and level the surface.
3. Draw directly on the clay with a sharp tool, erasing and redrawing until your design is resolved.
4. Decide which areas will be cut away, and which areas will be built up by adding bits of clay.
5. Gradually refine the carving. As the clay slowly dries to the leather-hard stage, it will become easier to carve neatly.
6. Add wreath and crest.
7. Add mantle by applying bits of clay and pressing them into leaf designs with your tool.
8. Trim outside edge.
9. Dry slowly.
10. Stain the greenware with diluted underglaze, and gently wipe off raised parts so stain remains in the recesses and hollows.
11. Fire to cone 06.

CONCLUSION:

Now that students have carved their own heraldic emblems, how could they translate it into a graphic design that could be used on a T-shirt or a hat? What other adaptation of this sign to their personal possessions could be made? (See Figure 2–14 for an actual studio art project.)

FOLLOW-UP

Look for crests and insignia in the ordinary world: schools and colleges use specific seals, and some chrome emblems on cars imply the heraldic source of automobile trademarks.

CREATIVE WRITING

Pretend to inhabit a home with a newly sculpted insignia set into its gate. Write a letter to a foreign friend explaining the meaning of your identifying coat of arms.

Figure 2-14. Studio art project. Personal heraldic insignia carved in clay includes bees, stars, an oak tree, a crown, and a mantle of leafy vines. (Artwork by Susan Hogan.)

Name _____ Date _____

Vocabulary Worksheet for Ireland

Look up the definitions of these words in a dictionary, write the definition, and then use the word in writing a sentence about Ireland. Use a separate sheet of papaer for this activity.

abbey	insignia
An Tur Gloine	lead caming
Anglo	mantle
Arts & Crafts Movement	megalith
blazonry	motte and bailey
book shrines	neo-Gothic
Celtic Revival	nuclei
chalice	pagan
charge	Palladian
crest	potato famine
dolmen	resurgence
Druidic	stone tracery
embossing	stuccowork
field	thatched
filigree	translucent
Gaelic	turrets
Georgian architecture	veneration
illiterate	wrought

Geography Worksheet for Ireland

Look up the answers to these questions and issues in world atlases and encyclopedias. Use the back of this sheet if you need more space.

- What is the effect of the Gulf Stream on the weather and climate of Ireland?

  _____

  _____

- Describe the border that divides the island into Northern Ireland and the Republic of Ireland, and name the six counties of Northern Ireland.

  _____

  _____

- Locate the source of the River Shannon, and describe the main features of its path to the Atlantic.

  _____

  _____

- Plan a trip along Ireland's Atlantic coast, describing the locations of the bays, peninsulas, and islands you would pass. Include a description of the wildlife that inhabits this region.

  _____

  _____

- How are peat bogs formed, and how are they farmed?

  _____

  _____

- Where is the Burren located, and what are its distinguishing features?

  _____

  _____

Geography Worksheet for Ireland (continued)

- Choose one county of Ireland's twenty-six, and write a detailed description of its characteristic landscape.

  _____

  _____

- What do we know of the geological formation of this island by glacial action?

  _____

  _____

- What are drumlins, where are they located, and how were they formed?

  _____

  _____

- What are the names of the individual Aran Islands?

  _____

  _____

- Locate wetlands on the map—the loughs and their surrounding marshes and rivers— and explain their importance for the nation's ecological balance.

  _____

  _____

- Name the different oceans and seas surrounding Ireland.

  _____

  _____

- Locate Ireland's large cities. Can you say why, in terms of geography, these population centers developed where they did?

  _____

  _____

Related Assignments for Ireland

1. **History.** Make a timeline of the sequence of events that is the history of Ireland.

2. **Art History.** Research the works of Irish painters, including Jack Yeats, George Barret, Philip Hussey, Augustus Burke, Paul Henry, and Louis LeBrocquy.

3. **Celtic Christian Crosses.** Examine and compare the carved stone crosses bound with a circular wheel. Study the scenes from the Bible carved into the famous crosses at Cashel and Clonmacnois in the ninth and tenth centuries.

4. **Drama.** World-famous Irish playwrights to read include George Bernard Shaw, J. M. Synge, Oscar Wilde, Sean O'Faolin, and Samuel Beckett.

5. **Literature.** Read James Joyce: *Portrait of the Artist as a Young Man*, *The Dubliners*; W. B. Yeats: *Collected Poems*; Jonathan Swift: *Gulliver's Travels*.

6. **Biography**
   - James Joyce
   - Samuel Beckett
   - W. B. Yeats
   - Lady Gregory
   - Saint Patrick
   - Jonathan Swift
   - Strongbow
   - J. M. Synge

7. **Travelogue.** Plan a historical tour of Ireland, focusing on the interpretation of visible remains of historical events.

8. **Architecture.** Make a detailed study of Georgian and Palladian styles of architecture in the eighteenth and nineteenth centuries.

9. **Glass Artisanry.** Study the manufacture of glass at the Waterford crystal factory, the largest glass factory in the world.

10. **Follow the News.** Report on the continuing conflict in Northern Ireland between Protestant majority and Catholic minority and describe Northern Ireland's effort to become an independent nation from the United Kingdom.

RESOURCES FOR TEACHING

BOOKS

Biesty, Stephen. *Cross-Section Castle*. London: Dorling Kindersley, 1994. (Many very detailed drawings show all aspects of life in a fourteenth-century European castle.)

Bowe, Nicola Gordon. *Harry Clarke*. Black Rock: Irish Academic Press, 1989.

Meehan, Bernard. *The Book of Kells, an Illustrated Introduction to the Manuscript in Trinity College Dublin*. London: Thames and Hudson, 1994.

Crespo, Michael. *Watercolor Day-by-Day*. New York: Watson-Guptill, 1987.

Neubecker, Ottfried. *Heraldry, Sources, Symbols, Meaning*. New York: McGraw-Hill, 1976.

Yeats, W. B., ed. *Irish Fairy and Folk Tales*. New York: Modern Library, 1994.

PERIODICALS

Ireland of the Welcomes, published bi-monthly by the Irish Tourist Board, Baggot Street Bridge, Dublin 2, Ireland. Phone: (800) 876-6336.

The World of Hibernia, published quarterly by World of Hibernia, Inc., 305 Madison Avenue, Suite 411, New York, NY 10165. Phone: (800) 458-3473.

VIDEOTAPES

Touring Ireland, Questar Home Video, 1991.

Ireland, A Writer's Island, ("see the beauty of Ireland through the eyes of her most famous writers"), Rego Irish Records & Tapes Inc., 1990.

NATIONAL TOURIST BOARD

Irish Tourist Board
395 Park Avenue
New York, NY 10035
(212) 418-0800

BOOKSTORE

Irish Book Shop
580 Broadway
New York, NY 10012
(212) 274-1923

MUSEUM RESOURCES

National Museum of Ireland
Kildare Street
Dublin 2, Ireland

BIBLIOGRAPHY

Allcock, Hubert. *Heraldic Design, Its Origins, Ancient Forms and Modern Usage*. New York: Tudor Publishing Co., 1962.

Armitage, E. Liddall. *Stained Glass*. Newton, MA: Charles T. Branford Co., 1959.

Baedecker's Ireland. New York: Prentice Hall Press, 1994.

Cahill, Thomas. *How the Irish Saved Civilization, The Untold Story of Ireland's Heroic Role from the Fall of Rome to the Rise of Medieval Europe*. New York: Doubleday, 1995.

Crespo, Michael. *Watercolor Day-by-Day*. New York: Watson-Guptill, 1987.

de Breffny, Brian. *Heritage of Ireland*. London: Weidenfeld & Nicolson, 1980.

Harbison, Peter, Homan Potterton, and Jeanne Sheehy. *Irish Art and Architecture, From Prehistory to the Present*. London: Thames & Hudson, 1978.

Illustrated Guide to Ireland, Sandy Shepherd, Project Editor, London: Reader's Digest Association Ltd., 1992.

Knopf Guides. *Ireland*. New York: Alfred A. Knopf, 1995.

Michelin Green Guide. *Ireland*. London: Harrow, 1992.

O'Comain, Micheal. *The Poolbeg Book of Irish Heraldry*. Dublin: Poolbeg, 1991.

O'Donovan, Donal. "Loughrea Cathedral," *Ireland of the Welcomes*, Vol. 33, March-April 1984, 41-45.

Sheehy, Terence. *Ireland and Her People*. New York: Greenwich House, 1983.

Southwest America: The Hopi

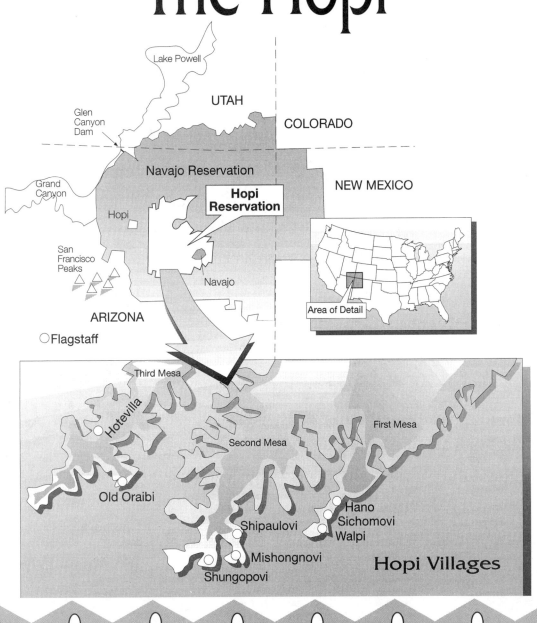

Lake Powell

UTAH

Glen Canyon Dam

COLORADO

Navajo Reservation

NEW MEXICO

Grand Canyon

Hopi

Hopi Reservation

San Francisco Peaks

Navajo

Area of Detail

ARIZONA

○ Flagstaff

Third Mesa

Hotevilla

First Mesa

Second Mesa

Old Oraibi

Hano
Sichomovi
Walpi

Shipaulovi

Mishongnovi

Shungopovi

Hopi Villages

A BRIEF HISTORY OF THE HOPI

The Hopi village of Old Oraibi in northern Arizona is the oldest continuously inhabited settlement in North America. The Hopi people have been living there since they chose to establish themselves on Black Mesa in about 1200 A.D. This remote and isolated place has been a successful choice of habitat, for it has helped protect the Hopi way of life from the intrusion of outsiders. The Hopi people have the distinction of being the Native American group that has been the least affected by colonization and assimilation into the world of "the white man." (See Figure 3–1.)

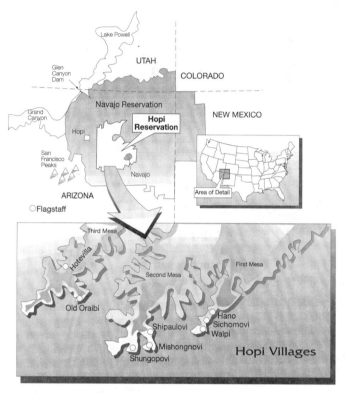

Figure 3-1. Map of the Hopi. This is a simplified locator map for quick reference. Students can look up a more detailed map of the Hopi reservation in a world atlas or history book.

When the Anasazi ("the ancient ones") deserted their cliff dwellings at Mesa Verde, Betatakin, Keet Seel, and other sites in the Four Corners region of the southwestern United States, between 1100 and 1200 A.D., they dispersed in small groups to settle at new locations. Similar traditions can be identified among the Hopi, the Zuni, and the different Pueblo peoples of the Rio Grande valley, but each of these groups has developed distinctive languages, arts, and customs in the past eight or nine centuries. The Navajo, whose reservation now surrounds the Hopi and whose population outnumbers them, are much later arrivals, coming into the area from much farther north in about the fifteenth century.

In recent years, Navajo population growth and the need for more grazing land to support more people has caused encroachment on the traditional Hopi land. This threat from the outside is only the latest conflict over territory in recent centuries. Early on, the Hopi were threatened by the neighboring Ute and Apache. In the seventeenth century, they forcefully resisted the Spanish Catholic missionaries, and they have been tenaciously holding out against pressure by the expanding Navajo population to absorb Hopi land.

The Hopi are a people of peace who are still maintaining their tradition—against all odds—of centuries of living in harmony with their natural environment of earth and sky. Twelve Hopi villages are situated on top of the 600-foot cliffs that rise to support First Mesa, Second Mesa, and Third Mesa. (See Figure 3–2.) In recent years new homes have been built at the foot of the mesas where the cornfields are located, in the midst of a vast and seemingly barren stretch of landscape that looks like it will support very little. Corn is the staple crop, honored in Hopi tradition and ceremony as the source of all life. Rituals are practiced throughout the year to connect their agriculture to the forces of nature—to rainfall and to abundant harvest. Hopi rely on the support of kachinas—spirit intermediaries between humanity and divine powers—for help in sustaining close relationships of family and community.

Figure 3-2. 1882 photograph of Mishongnovi Pueblo shows Shipaulovi in the distance. (Photograph by John K. Hillers. Courtesy of Museum of New Mexico, #2617.)

The Native American peoples have always used available natural resources to make the necessary utensils of daily living. Hopi still practice the traditional craft arts of pottery, basketry, weaving, wood carving, and jewelry. The Hopi arts have developed great sophistication in response to wide popularity in the world art market. The functional arts have always expressed their close relationship to the natural environment, and have become an integral factor in the maintenance of community. The Hopi commitment to close harmony with nature and with each other demands constant hard work to maintain.

WORKING WITH CLAY

Hopi pottery is an art of the earth, created from local earth material and always in a round form. A wheel has never been used in making these functional earthenware vessels for gathering food and water, cooking, and storage. Though this ancient craft has always been women's work in the Hopi culture—a domestic art essential for the survival of the community—in the twentieth century, men have also become clay sculptors and pot makers.

All pottery was considered sacred. Not only basically useful for storage and cooking of food, it has always been part of the paraphernalia in religious ceremonies. Pots were customarily buried with the dead until the Spanish Catholics came along and forbade such practices in their attempt to convert the Hopi to Christianity. Nonetheless the Hopi, as well as the other Pueblo groups, tenaciously maintained their own heritage of symbolic designs: feathers and birds, sky and cloud bands, circles, stars, suns, the four directions, and stylized animal and plant motifs.

The quality of this pottery had slowly declined from about 1700 on, but in 1885 the art form received a strong renewal. Archaeological excavations at Sikyatki on First Mesa uncovered old pottery pieces. Nampeyo of Hano, wife of one of the archaeological workers, visited the excavation and began to make drawings of the designs on the newly unearthed pots. From then on, all of her work incorporated modified Sikyatki symbols. When pictures of Nampeyo's brilliant ceramic works were published by the Santa Fe Railroad to promote Western tourism, she became famous. To this day, Nampeyo's family and her descendants have continued the tradition of pottery decoration based on the ancient Sikyatki designs. (See Figures 3–3A and B, 3–4A and B, and 3–5A and B.)

Figures 3-3A and 3-3B. Hopi pottery made by Tonita Nampeyo; 5-3/4 inches wide by 4 inches high. (Courtesy of Penfield Gallery, Albuquerque, New Mexico.)

Figures 3-4A and 3-4B. Hopi pottery made by Rachel Samie Nampeyo; 3 inches wide by 2-1/2 inches high. (Courtesy of Penfield Gallery, Albuquerque, New Mexico.)

Figures 3-5A and 3-5B. Hopi pottery made by Priscilla Namingha Nampeyo; 3 inches wide by 6 inches high. (Courtesy of Penfield Gallery, Albuquerque, New Mexico.)

MAKING POTTERY IN THE HOPI STYLE

For these projects in clay, the teacher's basic working knowledge of ceramics is assumed. Many excellent books are available that include pictorial explanations of press-molding, pinching pots, and building with coils. The technical aspects of underglazing, glazing, and firing have been thoroughly covered in many easily available reference books on ceramic craft.

For Hopi-style work, low-fire (cone 06) white clay is recommended. Underglazes can be painted onto the greenware before the bisque firing. The underpainted designs can be augmented with glaze painting before the final firing.

Basic pottery tools are sufficient. Plastic bags are useful for keeping the work from drying out too fast. Rigid paper plates without plastic or wax coating are great for press molds for the canteen project.

Project 3–1: Forming Clay Bowls in Press Molds

This is a simple process of clay forming with rewarding results. It is good to get the feel of the clay, and several bowls and pots can be simply formed on which students can start exploring different surface designs.

PREPARATION

Motivate the students by showing pictures of Hopi pots. Discuss the function of the pottery and the symbolic meaning of the sky motifs.

MATERIALS

- shallow bowls to use for molds (paper, wood, bisqued ware, and plaster bowls can be used for press molds. Glass and plastic bowls will stick to the clay. Place knit fabric between glass or plastic and clay, so the clay will easily pull away from it as it dries.)
- white low-fire clay (cone 06)
- electric kiln
- tools to smooth the surfaces
- a damp sponge
- newspapers
- plastic bags
- small boards to hold the ware while it dries
- brushes and black underglaze for decoration

PROCEDURE

1. Wedge a workable size lump of clay. Then press it with fingers and palms into a flatter form.
2. Press the thin clay slab into a wooden bowl, gradually flattening and smoothing with a tool.
3. Let it stiffen briefly. As it slightly dries and shrinks away from the mold, smooth the rim.
4. When stiff enough to handle, invert the mold onto a folded sheet of newspaper on a board.
5. Smooth the outer surface of the bowl and dry it slowly, keeping it lightly covered with plastic so it won't crack. The newspaper underneath it will absorb some of the moisture and contract as the bowl gradually dries and shrinks.

CONCLUSION

Have students make a few bowls of different sizes and depths. In this way they will become familiar with forming and smoothing the clay. They will also have several bowls on which they can explore different possibilities of surface design.

FOLLOW-UP

While the bowls are drying (a day or two), take this time to study traditional Hopi design motifs.

CREATIVE WRITING

Pretend you are a member of the archaeological team that unearthed pottery pieces at Sikyatki on First Mesa. How do you feel about this discovery? How will you convince others that this is an important discovery?

Design Process for Painting Circular Motifs

Circular designs inside Sikyatki and Hopi bowls are abstractions of natural forms. (See Figure 3–6 for sample motifs.) Birds, feathers, and sky bands are the subject for an endless array of variations. Feathers and winged creatures—birds, insects, moths, and butterflies—symbolize communication of the human with the spirit powers. Sun disks are also used inside bowls. The outside borders around the rims are sky bands symbolic of clouds, rain, and flying birds. Thunderbirds and thunderclouds appear as stylized geometry.

Students can identify variations of the different symbols and select one or two to modify and use for painting their pottery.

Using black paint and brushes to paint on newspapers gives the students plenty of latitude to discover their own interpretations of the Hopi designs. Have them paint until they feel relaxed and confident, and keep on painting until they have reached a satisfactory resolution of a selected theme to paint on their pots.

Project 3–2: Forming Hopi-style Coil Pots

PREPARATION

Refer to books on hand-building with clay, such as *The Big Book of Clay* (see "Resources for Teaching") for techniques and illustrations of the process of coil construction.

MATERIALS

- shallow round forms (bowls) to use for pukis (paper, wood, bisqued ware, and plaster bowls can be used as a "puki" to support the coiled base of a pot while building it)
- white low-fire clay (cone 06)
- electric kiln
- tools to smooth the surfaces

Figure 3-6. Sample Sikyatki motifs. (Reprinted from Prehistoric Hopi Pottery Designs by permission of Dover Publications.)

- a damp sponge
- newspapers
- plastic bags
- small boards to hold the ware while it dries
- brushes and black underglaze for decoration
- sandstone (or plastic scouring pad)
- quartzite river pebble (or stainless steel spoon)

PROCEDURE

1. Begin with a base of clay pressed into the mold, called a puki, to hold it securely.
2. Roll clay between your hands to produce a coil.
3. Lay the coil around the edge of the base, pinching and smoothing it into place.
4. Continue with several coils to form the walls of the vessel, developing the form by inclining inwards or outwards. Refer to source pictorial material in books on elementary pottery-forming for guidance in building basic pot forms.
5. When the desired form is reached, smooth the surface by scraping it with a tool (Hopi potters use a piece of gourd rind) and supporting the work with the other hand inside the pot. Patient smoothing with the tool will obliterate the coil pattern.
6. Keep adding more coils to build the pot to a desired height. If you work small, however, you will have enough time and material to try forming more than one coil pot.
7. Dry the pots slowly (cover loosely).
8. At the leather-hard stage, scrape the surface with a sherd or tool to further smooth and refine it.
9. When fully dry, smooth the surface with a piece of sandstone (or a plastic scouring pad).
10. After sanding, slightly moisten the surface and use a highly polished quartzite river pebble (or the back of a stainless steel spoon) to burnish the surface until it is smooth and shiny. This slow process requires patience.
11. While burnishing, begin to imagine the painting you will apply to the surface.
12. Prepare to paint the pot by warming up on paper, because your carefully burnished clay surfaces can be ruined by water, erasures, and other corrections!

CONCLUSION

Paint designs on dry pots and bisque fire them. In doing several of these (small) pots, students can really begin to explore how the form and the painting work together. (See Figures 3–7, 3–8A, and 3–8B.)

FOLLOW-UP

When the pots are on display, discuss the value of traditional pots as artifacts and as art, and how their function has changed from simple domestic use to a product for sale.

CREATIVE WRITING

Write about the process of building these pots from start to finish, comparing your experience with that of Hopi potters.

Figure 3-7. Studio art project. Bowl made with coils of clay has typical flat shoulders. The butterfly design from Sikyatki pottery is still used by Hopi potters. (Artwork by Susan Hogan.)

Project 3–3: Making a Hopi Canteen

Canteens are clay bottles used to carry water to drink in the fields. They have a narrow neck, or short spout from which to drink, and two handles from which the canteen can be suspended from the shoulder by a thin strap, or hung on a wall. Since the clay they are made of is porous, it has a cooling effect (by evaporation) on the water it holds. Clay canteens have been made and used by all of the Pueblo peoples of Arizona and New Mexico for centuries.

PREPARATION

Discuss the importance of water in the arid environment of the Hopi, and point out the ways that water, as rain, is honored and thanked in ceremonial dances.

MATERIALS

- small uncoated paper plates or shallow wooden bowls to use for molds
- electric kiln
- white low-fire clay (cone 06)
- damp sponges
- clay modeling tools

Figure 3-8A. Bowl by Hopi potter Dextra Nampeyo, First Mesa; 7-3/4 inches wide by 3-1/2 inches high. (Courtesy of Penfield Gallery, Albuquerque, New Mexico.)

Figure 3-8B. Bowl by Hopi potter Mark Tahbo; 6 inches wide by 3-1/2 inches high. (Courtesy of Penfield Gallery, Albuquerque, New Mexico.)

- newspapers
- plastic bags
- small boards to hold the ware while it dries
- brushes and black underglaze for decoration

PROCEDURE

1. Wedge a lump of clay. Then flatten it with palms and fists.
2. Press the clay into two (unwaxed) paper plates, and allow it to stiffen for about 15 minutes. The paper draws the moisture out of the clay and makes it easier to handle.
3. When these shallow molded bowls shrink slightly away from the plates, carefully pull them out and join the two together at the edges.
4. Trim the edges evenly, and use slip to glue the two pieces together. Let the clay stiffen a bit before smoothing the round seam with a pottery tool.
5. Cut a small one-inch circular or oval hole for the spout.
6. To construct the spout, cut a strip of slab and form a short cylinder that fits into the hole. Work it securely into place with fingers and tools.
7. Make handles by rolling out coils and attaching them with slip. Make sure the handles are thick enough to hold the canteen when it is suspended by the strap.
8. Handle the hollow form carefully and dry it slowly.

CONCLUSION

Refer to Project 3–2 for painting. Students can paint designs with underglazes onto both sides of the canteens before bisque firing. After the ware is bisqued, they can further develop their designs before applying clear satin glaze (diluted 50 percent with water) to the canteens with a sponge. A final glaze firing will complete the project. Figure 3–9 shows two actual studio art projects.

FOLLOW-UP

Attach hanging straps of twine or leather thongs to the canteens, and hang a display of the work.

CREATIVE WRITING

Write a press release for your class exhibit of Hopi-style pottery. Explain the function and significance of the traditional style to a prospective audience.

HOPI MESAS AND VILLAGES

Shongapovi, Mishongnovi, Shipaulovi . . . the Hopi village names of northern Arizona evoke the remote and mysterious atmosphere of the place. Their distance from typical American life and the apparent emptiness of their surrounding terrain have helped protect these centuries-old habitations from being colonized and absorbed by mainstream American culture. The

Figure 3-9. Studio art project. Canteens made of clay pressed into molds, painted with variations of traditional Sikyatki bird images. (Artwork by Susan Hogan.)

Hopi villages of First Mesa, Second Mesa, and Third Mesa were constructed of stone and mud hundreds of years ago in the manner of the ancient now-ruined dwellings of the Anasazi, still visible at Betatakin, Keet Seel, and other archaeological sites in northern Arizona. This natural architecture in harmony with the harsh terrain has sheltered the Hopi since they selected this distinctive northern Arizona location to protect the people's peaceful lifestyle from the surrounding warlike tribes of the Apache, the Ute, and the Navaho.

The privacy of the communities is still maintained today to protect and preserve the integrity of the Hopi way from outside intrusion. Photography by outsiders is prohibited. Visitors to some of the Hopi villages are requested to enter only with Hopi guides or tour groups. The Hopi Cultural Center on Second Mesa is a museum–motel–restaurant–gift shop complex that exhibits Hopi customs, arts, and history, and offers pottery, kachina dolls, silverwork, and paintings for sale.

Project 3–4: Sculpting a Clay Relief of Mesa-top Villages

In this relief sculpture studio project, students can extend their experience with clay to a more complex pictorial work. This is a study of the way in which these man-made towns have been inspired by the semi-arid mountainous desert that supports them, and built in an organic relationship, so to speak, to their surrounding terrain. (See Figure 3–10.)

Figure 3-10. Hopi village of Walpi on Second Mesa in 1921. (Photograph by Bortell. Courtesy of Museum of New Mexico, #2640.)

PREPARATION

Look for pictorial resources of Hopi villages. The *Handbook of North American Indians*, available in the reference section of many libraries, gives aerial views of some of the villages. Junior books on the Hopi are also a good source for pictures. Photocopy pictures of the mesas and villages and enlarge them. Each student will receive two or three copies. They can study the design aspects of the structures by using pencil and eraser directly on the photocopies. Have them emphasize forms by darkening with the pencil, and use the eraser to lighten contrasting areas to develop the three-dimensional representation with light and dark, working on the picture until reaching a sense of resolution.

MATERIALS

- white low-fire clay (cone 06)
- electric kiln
- clay modeling tools
- a damp sponge
- newspapers
- plastic bags
- wareboards to support each work-in-progress (can be thin plywood or masonite, approximately 12" x 15")
- brushes and underglazes or stains for painting the greenware

PROCEDURE

1. Roll out a slab of clay about 1/4 inch thick. Approximately 11" x 14" is a good dimension because it is manageable, can be built up in some detail, and will not warp too much as it dries.

2. Place each slab on a piece of thin plastic on a wareboard approximately the same size.

3. Begin work by sketching the mesa village scene into the clay with a sharp tool. The drawing can be easily changed and modified as you work.

4. When you have resolved the preliminary drawing in the clay, start building up some areas by beginning to add bits of clay and smoothing them with the spatula.

5. By gradually building up walls and carving out open spaces, the design will evolve through several stages of development.

6. To finish the surfaces, the buildings can be smoothed, and the surrounding terrain of the mesas and cliffs can be a rougher rockier texture. Actual rough stones can be pressed into the clay to make stone texture.

7. Be sure to dry these relief sculptures slowly (to keep the clay from warping and cracking) by keeping them loosely covered. Plastic bags are useful for protecting them at this stage.

CONCLUSION

The pieces can be stained with oxides or earth colors in the greenware stage before bisque-firing them to cone 06. Figure 3–11 shows an actual studio art project.

Figure 3-11. Studio art project. The village of Walpi is a dramatic inspiration for this mesa sculpture of white clay, which has been bisque fired and painted with watercolors. (Artwork by Susan Hogan.)

FOLLOW-UP

This project is effective at any level of sophistication, and can be used to study other earth architecture or archaeological sites of the Southwest.

CREATIVE WRITING

Imagine the experience of living in this place you have depicted. Express in words the feeling of living so close to earth and sky, stones and clouds, undistracted by the crowds, noise, and clutter of dense population.

HOPI SILVERWORK

The most popular body ornaments of the early Southwestern peoples were apparently the pendants made of shell with applied mosaics of tiny stones, particularly turquoise. Shell jewelry, beads made of drilled stone, and etched, carved stone pendants are found in all archaeological sites of the region.

Silver was brought to the Southwest Indians by the Spanish in the seventeenth century. The Navajo were the first to learn the craft of silverwork from the Mexicans in the mid-nineteenth century, and it was the Navajo who taught silverworking to the Zuni people, who taught the craft to the Hopi in 1898! At first, silver artisans working on Second Mesa and Third Mesa hammered silver coins into ornaments that they decorated by stamping them with designs copied from Mexican leatherwork, following the Navajo styles.

Hopi jewelers began working with sheet silver in the 1930s, and were encouraged by curators of Indian arts at the Museum of Northern Arizona in Flagstaff to develop a uniquely Hopi style. They began to use designs adapted from tribal textiles, basketry, and ceramics. White traders with the Indians, especially in Gallup, New Mexico, began to commercialize this Hopi jewelry.

Today, Hopi silverwork is identified with the overlay technique, described as follows: Cut out two identical pieces of sheet silver with a jeweler's saw. One is left plain; a silhouette design is cut out of the second piece. The two pieces are fluxed together, then oxidized, which turns them black. The top layer is polished, leaving the visible cut-out pattern black. Bracelets, pendants, bolos, and concha belts, as well as small sculptures, have become highly personal and expressive art forms based on this characteristic technique. (See Figure 3–12.) Kachina dances are sometimes portrayed in great detail on silver medallions to make up a concha belt. Traditional clan symbols—corn, rain, clouds, eagles, lightning, sun, kiva steps, bear paws—are often used in contemporary Hopi silver jewelry art. Kokopelli, the humpbacked flute player of Hopi mythology, is such a popular character with tourists that his image is used not only on bracelets, pendants, bolos, and concha belts, but also on almost every product imaginable.

It was Charles Loloma (1921–1991), a Hopi from Hotevilla, who stimulated the breakthrough from traditional native jewelry to world-class contemporary style. As a high school student in the 1930s, Loloma showed great promise in painting and drawing classes. After discharge from the Army after World War II, he studied ceramics at Alfred University on the G.I. Bill. He worked in Scottsdale, Arizona for many years making and selling pottery, and eventually began experimenting with jewelry.

Figure 3-12. Bolo of silver overlay is a stylized sun face, made by Lonovu Keicheve.

Loloma interpreted the landscape of the Hopi mesas of his childhood in distinctive bracelets set with all kinds of stones, which he called "height bracelets." He became a well-known participant in official Indian art conferences and institutes, advocating greater individual expression and demanding greater recognition. Loloma met fashion designers and traveled to Paris and fashion shows all over Europe where his jewelry was presented. This wide exposure expanded his jewelry designs and brought him fame and fortune. Eventually Loloma built a studio in Hotevilla on Third Mesa. Two of his nieces served as his apprentices, helping to produce the quantity of his jewelry that popular acclaim demanded. Their work is now known as *Sonwai*, the word for "feminine beauty" in Hopi.

Project 3–5: Making Aluminum Concha Belts in Hopi Style

Concha belts were originally made by the Navajo in the 1800s out of heavy silver. The word *concha* comes from the Spanish word for shell. Conchas are silver disks that are threaded or strung together to make belts. Hopi silversmiths today have developed a very intricate overlay technique with which they depict kachina dances and ceremonies in great detail on each concha for a unique belt.

PREPARATION

Interlocking design elements are black and silver in a dynamic balance of positive and negative. Translate the design elements of silver overlay—black silhouette on silver surface—into disks made of black cardboard and aluminum cutouts.

Students can either use traditional Hopi symbols for this project or invent their own. They could repeat the same design on each "concha" or create a series of seven or eight different conchas.

Figure 3-13. Studio art project. Belt of seven round "conchas" that imitate the look of silver overlay in heavy aluminum foil and black cardboard. (Artwork by Susan Hogan.)

Collect recycled boxes, such as cereal boxes and cracker boxes, which are the right weight and thickness for making these pieces.

MATERIALS

- disposable aluminum pie plates or roasting pans (can be purchased in the supermarket; can be flattened out with the back of a spoon)
- paper, pencils, marking pen, scissors
- one box (see Preparation) per student
- gel medium or white glue
- a damp sponge
- black paint, brushes, water containers
- felt or leather strips, 1/2-inch wide and 26 to 30 inches long

PROCEDURE

1. Paint your box black with acrylic paint or poster paint, and set it aside to dry.
2. With paper and pencil, develop one motif into a simple but strong positive/negative image.
3. Cut out a matching set of seven or eight disks of the painted cardboard.
4. Cut a "silver" overlay pattern design out of paper.
5. Place the paper pattern on aluminum, draw around it, and cut it out.
6. Make as many repeats of the design as you want to put into the belt.
7. Glue each aluminum element to a black disk with gel medium. Blot extra overflow glue with a damp sponge, then let disks dry.
8. Arrange the series of disks about an inch apart on a strip of black felt, or a leather strip, and glue each one in place with gel medium (or white glue). Let dry.

CONCLUSION

Students can model their concha belts for each other, giving a brief description of their work in the process. Figure 3–13 shows an actual studio art project.

FOLLOW-UP

- A variety of additional shapes for necklaces, pendants, bracelets, or pins can be cut out of the heavy foil with scissors, embossed, and punched with tools.
- This experience of crafting jewelry designs in heavy aluminum can be followed up by actually working in sheet silver. It is relatively expensive, but if students are prepared and eager to try silverworking, sheets can be ordered from school art supply catalogs. (A less expensive alternative is alpaca, which is available in metalcraft catalogs.)

CREATIVE WRITING

Write a dialogue between a jewelry artisan and a trader, discussing where and how the work will be marketed.

HOPI KACHINAS

It has been said that kachina dances of the Southwest are the most genuine American art form. Certainly the kachina dolls and the dancers they represent are one of the most popular and well known of Native American arts. (See Figure 3–14.) Kachinas are spirit beings that bring rain and abundant harvests of corn to the Hopi people. They inhabit the San Francisco Peaks near Flagstaff, Arizona. In November every year the kachinas emerge from their home to visit the Hopi people, whose ceremonial year is arranged to express their relationship with these spirit beings. Hopi believe that their devoted communication with the kachina spirits is the essential part of the Hopi role to caretake the earth on behalf of all mankind.

Figure 3-14. Kachina carving of crib doll is very flat and simple, but conveys specific character. (Courtesy of Charles and Leslie Donaldson, Scottsdale, Arizona.)

Male secret societies promulgate and sponsor the kachina ceremonial year. In a kiva (an underground ceremonial chamber), they are initiated into rituals of song and dance. The men in these religious societies prepare the masks and other dance regalia. Kachina masks have the power to confer identity with the kachina spirits when worn by initiated men.

There are about 200 different kachina characters in the Hopi pantheon—rain and sun spirits, animals, ogres, and clowns. New ones are sometimes added, and old ones can be eliminated. Each kachina of these vital spirit forces who watch over the people and control their destiny has a function and an identity expressed by a unique combination of symbolic signs.

Discipline, clowning, fertility of the earth, corn, and prayers for good harvests all through the planting time are expressed by elaborately costumed dancers in regular ceremonies from the winter solstice to the "Home Dance" in July, when the kachinas return to their mountain abode in the San Francisco Peaks.

Kachina dolls are intended to be educational. They are made to teach children about the natures of the many different kachinas. Carvers use cottonwood roots gathered in the arroyos, or dry riverbeds, for carving the dolls. On the complete carving is painted a basecoat of white kaolin (white earth). Poster colors in full intensity are used over the base in depicting the identifying designs and masks, then the appropriate clothes and feathers.

At the end of the nineteenth century, Indian traders sold dolls to collectors, and began to popularize them as curiosities. The older dolls are simpler (see Figure 3–15) and there has

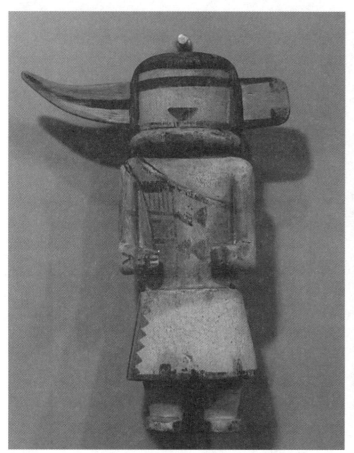

Figures 3-15. Antique kachinas. (Courtesy of Charles and Leslie Donaldson, Scottsdale, Arizona.)

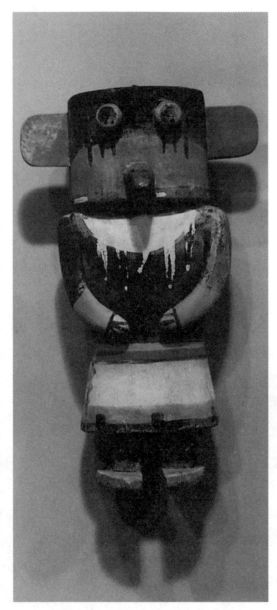
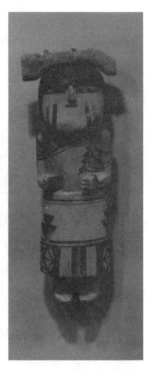

Figures 3-15. (continued)

been a gradual development in style for the expectations of the white market. The more recent carved kachinas have become more realistic—in proportions, articulation of limbs, more dynamic poses, and greater development of detail. (See Figure 3–16.) Now kachina carving has become a personal art form and a source of income for the artist, for sale to outsiders in the shops and trading posts in and near the Hopi mesas, and in the tourist centers in Santa Fe, Albuquerque, and Scottsdale.

Figure 3-16. Carving of an eagle kachina by Joseph Duwyenie shows how contemporary Hopi carving has evolved to fine detail and articulation, to satisfy the tastes of contemporary collectors. (Courtesy of Penfield Gallery, Albuquerque, New Mexico.)

Project 3–6: Making a Folio of Kachina Drawings

PREPARATION

Gather pictures of as many different kachinas as you can find. Encyclopedias, Southwestern art books and magazines, and children's books may be good sources for a wide variety of these images.

MATERIALS

- drawing pencils
- sketch paper
- colored pencils
- drawing paper with some texture (18" × 12" paper will encourage students to work relatively large and in detail)

PROCEDURE

1. Sketch several different kachinas for preliminary studies of the different visual characteristics of these figures.

2. Select one favorite kachina to study: in drawing, in research, and in writing. (*Teacher*: Try to assign a different kachina to each student.)

3. After doing preliminary sketches from your visual source material, use colored pencils to develop a detailed and finished drawing of a particular kachina.

4. Write an explanatory caption of the drawing on another piece of paper the same size.

CONCLUSION

Combine all student kachina drawings into a folio. The folio can be displayed by placing all the works in a sequence on a long table. Figure 3–17 shows an actual studio art project.

FOLLOW-UP

Now that the students have basic knowledge of traditional Hopi kachinas, show them reproductions of contemporary interpretations of the kachina image, which can be readily located in different Southwest art magazines and gallery advertisements.

CREATIVE WRITING

Discuss the possibilities of inventing a new kachina who could bring improvement to your own community. Write a description of the character, its appearance, personality, behavior, costume, mask, and function.

TABLITAS: HEADDRESSES FOR CEREMONIAL AND SOCIAL DANCES

Traditionally, the costumes and ritual items for ceremonial art of the Hopi are made by the men of the villages in their kivas. Historically, they have determinedly protected their ritual arts from the curious intrusions of not only pahanas (whites) but of other Native American groups as well. The Hopi distinguish clearly between sacred ceremonial dances, such as the Snake Dance, and the social dances performed in joy and friendship for their neighbors and visitors from the outside world.

Men, women, and children participate in the Buffalo Dance in the villages in January. The Butterfly Dance (See Figure 3–19.) is a joyful expression performed mainly by children in the late summer; the dance continues into a celebration of the harvest. Hopi social dances are not so deeply religious as the plaza dances of kachinas, and photography is permitted—by Hopi people only—on these festive occasions. The costume symbolism is not kept a secret, as it customarily is for the other ritual kachina dances.

Tablitas are flat, carved, and painted headdresses worn as part of ceremonial dance costumes. There are numerous styles of tablitas for various celebrations. The designs for the different headdresses are based on the symbolism of particular kachinas. Usually they show stylized geometric emblems for sky, clouds, thunder, lightning, and rain. Feathers are attached to the tips of the cloud symbols to transmit the ceremonial songs, dances, and prayers of human performers into the heavens.

Figure 3-17. Studio art project. Colored pencil drawing of Soyal kachina doll. (Artwork by Susan Hogan.)

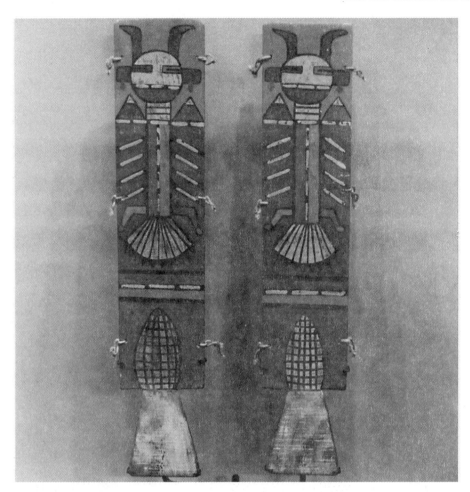

Figure 3-18. Hopi dance wands cut out of wood and painted with motifs of corn and a fertility god. (Courtesy of Charles and Leslie Donaldson, Scottsdale, Arizona.)

Figure 3-19. Hopi Butterfly Dancers performed at the Inter-Tribal Indian Ceremonial in Gallup, New Mexico, in 1935. (Photograph by Mullarky. Courtesy of Museum of New Mexico, #74785.)

Project 3–7: Making Painted Tablitas Cut Out of Foam Core

PREPARATION

Discuss the common features of the tablitas in the kachina doll pictures. Simplified symbolic motifs—rain and thunder, lightning, feathers, and birds—are repeated several times in composing a design.

MATERIALS

- foam core (at least 16- to 18-inch square) for each tablita
- pencils and sketch paper
- markers
- newspapers for patterns
- poster paints in primary colors and black
- rulers
- scissors
- brushes
- X-acto™ knife
- containers for water
- feathers (can be ordered from school art supply catalogs, or gathered where there are flocks of ducks, geese, or sea gulls)
- 18-inch ribbon or tie for each tablita (cut each length in two)

PROCEDURE

1. Make preliminary design studies for your tablita. (Figure 3–20 shows sample kachina designs.) Fold a piece of paper in half and sketch one half of the design; cut it out with scissors, and outline all design elements with a strong black line. Sketch several versions, varying the proportions and scale of the different elements. Color in the best ones with markers, using the primary colors (red, yellow, and blue) in full intensity.
2. Select the best one of these small studies to enlarge on a 24" × 30" piece of foam core (or rigid illustration board). Make a full-size paper pattern to trace around on the foam core.
3. The tablita can be painted with poster paints, which have the same bright colors and flat matte surface as authentic tablitas.
4. Cut out the design with an X-acto™ knife.
5. Attach a feather or two to each outer point of the design.
6. Glue a 9-inch (at least) length of ribbon to the inside edge at each side of the head for tying on the headdress.

CONCLUSION

Encourage students to model their tablitas. This group of painted dance headdresses will make a handsome display when arranged together on a panel or a wall. Figure 3–21 shows an actual studio art project.

Figure 3-20. Kachina dolls from the American Museum of Natural History. (Reprinted from *Southwestern Indian Designs* by permission of Dover Publications.)

FOLLOW-UP

Students can develop more personal elaborate headdresses and invent symbolic dances to perform in them.

CREATIVE WRITING

Imagine you are an eagle flying over the kachina dances in the villages on the Hopi mesas, and can see far into the past and the future. Describe what you see and feel.

Figure 3-21. Studio art project. Tablita cut out of foam core and painted yellow, red, black, white, and blue. Feathers, the finishing touch, were gathered at a duck pond. Raptor feathers are prohibited from use now, because eagles and hawks are endangered species. (Artwork by Susan Hogan.)

Vocabulary Worksheet for the Hopi

Look up the following vocabulary words in a dictionary, write the definition, and then use the word in a sentence about the Hopi. Use a separate sheet of paper for this activity

Anasazi	kaolin
apprentices	kiva
arroyo	mesa
assimilation	ogres
bisque	overlay
bolo tie	oxidized
canteen	pantheon
clans	puki
concha belt	relief
curators	reservation
encroachment	Sikyatki
fluxed	Sonwai
kachina	tablita

Geography Worksheet for the Hopi

Find the answers to these problems in world atlases and encyclopedias. Use the back of this sheet if you need more space.

- Study the practice of dry-land farming in this area of the United States. How is water distributed to make food crop cultivation possible?

  _____

  _____

- How does the relative scarcity of water become a crucial political and territorial issue in this arid area?

  _____

  _____

- Identify all the known sites of ancient settlements on a map of the Four Corners region.

  _____

  _____

- Locate the coal deposits on the Hopi territory and investigate the way this natural resource is being mined today.

  _____

  _____

- Draw a series of historical maps of Arizona to show the changes in how the land has been occupied, and how the boundary lines of the reservations have changed through the years.

- Compare the physical topography geography of Arizona with that of New Mexico. Refer to topographical maps in an atlas to see how the Rio Grande provides a direct water route into the heart of the country straight from Mexico, whereas all routes into Arizona from Mexico are blocked by transverse mountain ranges. What are the implications of this physical fact for the settlement of these two different states?

  _____

  _____

- Describe the vast geographical features of the Colorado River in Utah and Arizona, including dams and tributaries.

  _____

  _____

Related Assignments for the Hopi

1. **Biography**
   - Nampeyo of Hano
   - Qoyawayma, Polingaysi. *No Turning Back.* A true account of a Hopi Indian girl's struggle to bridge the gap between the world of her people and the world of the white man. Albuquerque: University of New Mexico Press, 1977.
   - Talayesva in Simmons, Leo W. (ed.). *Sun Chief: The Autobiography of a Hopi Indian.* New Haven: Yale University Press, 1942.

2. **Anthropology**. Compare designs, traditions, and ceremonies of other Native American Pueblo groups of the Southwest:
   - Acoma Pueblo
   - Taos Pueblo
   - Zuni Pueblo
   - Rio Grande Pueblos
   - Navajo Nation

3. **Art Appreciation**. Look up the work of these contemporary Hopi artists:
   - Fred Kabotie
   - Artist Hopid
   - Sonwai
   - Dan Namingha
   - Milland Lomakema

4. **Economics**. How do the Hopi sustain themselves economically in the modern world? Find out the facts about their employment, manufacturing, artisanry, agriculture, and U.S. Government support.

5. **History**. Research the legendary Seven Cities of Cibola and the encounter of Spanish explorers with the Southwestern Indians.

6. **Mythology**. Read the Hopi myths of origin and the creation of this world.

7. **Travelogue**. Plan a trip to the Southwest to study ancient architecture.

8. **Ecology**. How does the Native American philosophy of respect for the natural environment come into conflict with the capitalist economy of the United States?

RESOURCES FOR TEACHING

BOOKS

Allen, Laura Graves. *Contemporary Hopi Pottery*. Flagstaff: Museum of Northern Arizona, 1984.

Chavarria, Joachim. *The Big Book of Ceramics*. New York: Watson-Guptill Publications, 1994.

Cirillo, Dexter. *Southwestern Indian Jewelry*. New York: Abbeville Press, 1992.

Kabotie, Fred. *Fred Kabotie, Hopi Indian Artist*. Flagstaff: Museum of Northern Arizona, 1977.

Mullett, G. M. *Spider Woman Stories: Legends of the Hopi Indians*. Tucson: University of Arizona Press, 1979.

Northland Publishing, P.O. Box 1389, Flagstaff, AZ 86002–1389. This company offers a free catalog of their books about Southwest Native American arts, crafts, and culture. Phone: (800) 346-3257

PERIODICALS

American Indian Arts, published quarterly by American Indian Arts, Inc., 7314 E. Osborne Drive, Scottsdale, AZ 85251. Phone: (602) 994-5445.

Arizona Highways, published monthly by the Arizona Department of Transportation, 2039 W. Lewis Avenue, Phoenix, AZ 85009. Phone: 800-543-5432.

Native Peoples, published quarterly by Media Concepts Group, 5333 N. Seventh Street, Suite C-224, Phoenix, AZ 85014. Phone: (888) 262-8483.

VIDEOTAPE

Jacka, Jerry and Lois Essary Jacka. *Beyond Tradition: Contemporary Indian Art and Its Evolution*. Phoenix: Jacka Photography (P.O. Box 9043, Phoenix, AZ 85068), 1989.

MUSEUM RESOURCES

Museum of Northern Arizona
Highway 180 North
Flagstaff, AZ 86001
(520) 774-5211

Heard Museum
22 E. Monte Vista Road
Phoenix, AZ 85004
(602) 252-8840

Museum of New Mexico
107 W. Palace Avenue
Santa Fe, NM 87501
(505) 827-4468

National Museum of the American Indian
The George Gustav Heye Center
One Bowling Green
New York, NY 10004
(212) 283-2420

BIBLIOGRAPHY

Boelter, Homer H. *Portfolio of the Hopi Kachinas*. Hollywood, CA: Privately published, 1969.

Broder, Patricia Janis. *Hopi Painting*. New York: E. P. Dutton, 1978.

Fewkes, Jesse Walter. *Prehistoric Hopi Pottery Designs*. New York: Dover Publications, Inc., 1973.

Frank, Larry and Francis H. Harlow. *Historic Pottery of the Pueblo Indians, 1600–1800*. Atglen, PA: Schiffer, 1990.

Orban-Szontagh, Madeleine. *Southwestern Indian Designs*. New York: Dover Publications, Inc., 1992.

Page, Susanne and Jake. *Hopi*. New York: Harry N. Abrams, 1982.

Sears, Bryan P. *The Hopi Indians*. New York: Chelsea House, 1994.

Sherrow, Victoria. *The Hopi: Pueblo People of the Southwest*. Brookfield, CT: The Millbrook Press, 1993.

Sturtevant, William C. and Alfonzo Ortiz. *Handbook of North American Indians, Vol. 9: Southwest*. Washington, D.C.: U.S. Government Printing Office, 1990.

Tanner, Clara Lee. *Southwest Indian Craft Arts*. Tucson: University of Arizona Press, 1968.

Waters, Frank. *Book of the Hopi*. New York: Ballantine Books, 1969.

Weir, Bill. *Arizona Traveler's Handbook*. Chico, CA: Moon Publications, 1990.

Central America: The Maya

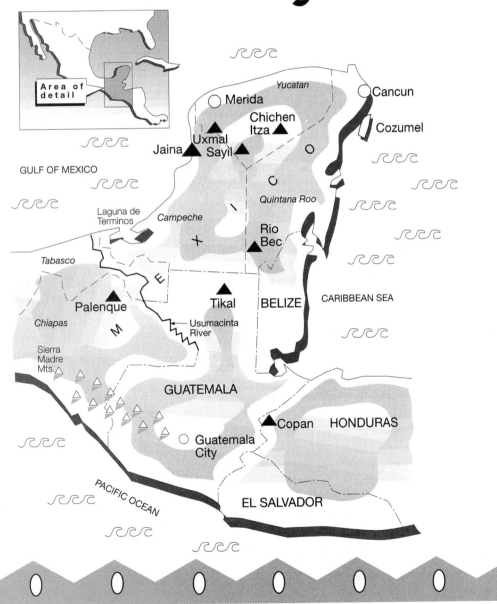

Area of detail

Yucatan

Merida ○

Chichen Itza ▲

Uxmal ▲
Jaina ▲ Sayil ▲

Cancun ○

Cozumel

GULF OF MEXICO

Laguna de Terminos

Campeche

Quintana Roo

Rio Bec ▲

Tabasco

Palenque ▲

Chiapas

Sierra Madre Mts. △

Tikal ▲

BELIZE

CARIBBEAN SEA

Usumacinta River

GUATEMALA

Copan ▲   HONDURAS

○ Guatemala City

PACIFIC OCEAN

EL SALVADOR

A BRIEF HISTORY OF THE MAYA

The civilization of the Maya, one of the most highly developed indigenous cultures of the American continents, had been declining long before Cortéz and other Spanish explorers entered the Mayan realm on their way to Central Mexico in the sixteenth century. Mayan settlements in the far eastern part of the land that is now Mexico were encountered by Cortéz on his way to conquer the Aztec empire in Central Mexico. On February 10, 1519, Hernan Cortéz sailed west from Cuba, following the route that first Córdoba and then Grijalva had taken to Mexico. His fleet of eleven ships with close to 900 men stopped at the island of Cozumel, just off the eastern coast of the Yucatan, for nearly three weeks, where Cortéz firmly established contact with the native Mayans, and set up discipline precedents for his soldiers and sailors. On March 4, the ships set sail for Veracruz and their destiny as conquerors of Montezuma's empire. (See Figure 4–1.)

Figure 4-1. Map of the Maya. This is a simplified locator map for quick reference. Students can look up a more detailed map of the Maya in a world atlas or history book.

Soon after discovery of the Mayan domain by the conquistadors came Spanish Catholic priests totally determined to convert "pagan" Native American souls to Christianity. Bishop Diego de Landa established Catholic missions in the Yucatan, and ordered the Mayan people to stop practicing the rituals of their own traditional religion. To enforce his harsh edicts against their religious observances, Bishop Landa destroyed their books and their art. Only four authentic Mayan books out of many thousands have survived both the frenzy of destruction by Catholic priests and the tropical climate. They are records of history, ritual, songs, legends, and calendrical notation, written and painted on long folded bark thinly coated with lime stucco. Known as codices, they bear the names of the cities where they are now located:

Madrid, Paris, Dresden, and Grolier (Mexico City). Eager as he had been to burn all records of Mayan civilization, Bishop Landa wrote carefully detailed accounts of their religious customs and way of life. He published these fascinating observations as *Relaciones de las Cosas de Yucatan* in 1560, a book that remains a unique source of information about this historic clash of Spanish and pre-Columbian worlds.

The great Mayan pyramid cities (see Figure 4–2) encountered by the Spaniards in the sixteenth century had been deserted for hundreds of years, and the remaining Maya population centers were such bitter enemies that they could not unite effectively against the force of the Spanish invasion. Desperate military battles for control of the population, land, and religion between the Mayans and the Spanish soldiers and missionaries began a centuries-long struggle for dominance by Spanish conquerors over indigenous Maya. The Spanish were ruthless in forcing the practice of Catholicism upon the Indians, and cruel in enslaving them to labor on the plantations they established.

Figure 4-2. The great pyramid at Uxmal, in the Puuc region of the Yucatan. (Photograph by Zebulon W. White.)

After the many centuries of turmoil and destruction, it is remarkable that anything of the traditional Maya identity survived. However, at least six million people of Mayan heritage and language now inhabit the region, from the Yucatan through the Peten jungle of northern Guatemala and Belize. Mayan villages are also densely clustered in highland Guatemala, on the slopes of the Sierra Madre. The lifestyles of these peasants continue many of the ways of farmers who lived during the time of Mayan high culture, known as the Classic era, from about 200 B.C.–900 A.D. In the present-day domestic architecture, the craft of weaving and manner of dress, the traditional crops grown for food (corn, beans, squash, and tortillas), and the rituals performed in honor of the same gods are evidence of continuance of ancient Mayan habits of connection to their ancestors, and the power of belief in their own customs, which have not been eradicated even after centuries of persecution.

MAYAN ARCHITECTURE

Rising throughout one of the great remaining tropical rain forests of the world is evidence of many unexplored ancient cities covered with jungle. (See Figure 4–3.) These hidden sites seem to cover the entire southern Yucatan peninsula, the northern Peten area of Guatemala, and much of western Belize. Infrared aerial photography has been revealing clear evidence of past land use: signs of raised fields and canal systems of an agriculture that was able to provide food for a very densely settled population. Traces remain of straight limestone highways, or sacbes, connecting many of these ancient places. Well before the Spaniards appeared in their world, the Maya abandoned their civilized cities. Sometime in the tenth century, they just walked away from the ceremonial centers, for reasons which are still a mystery to archaeologists.

Figure 4-3. Palenque ruins in Chiapas, Mexico. (Photograph by Zebulon W. White.)

Tourists from all over the world now visit the famous Mayan archaeological sites in the Yucatan, including Palenque, Uxmal, Kabah, Labna, and especially Chichen Itza. They walk through deserted and ruined architecture, plazas of temples, palaces, and pyramids covered with stone carvings of grotesque creatures, flowing linear arabesques that depict smoke and foliage, and millions of glyphs explaining the meaning of the images.

The limestone shelf that is the geological foundation of Maya terrain was the source of abundant easily-worked stone with which they built their cities. Buildings of limestone were covered with lime stucco, with which artisans sculpted images of animals, glyphs, streaming

Figure 4-4. The stylized limestone mask façade of a building at Hochob, Campeche, was reconstructed at the Museum of Anthropology in Mexico City.

foliage, and masks in relief. (See Figure 4–4.) When they were new, these buildings were painted brilliant reds, blues, greens, and yellows.

At the height of their civilization, during the thousand years between 200 B.C. and 800 A.D., the Classic Maya built pyramids to symbolize sacred mountains where the priests and kings were able to contact the Otherworld. The mythic cave within the mountain was ceremonially entered through the mouth of a monster—the giant masks which form the entryway. Snake and reptile imagery is seen everywhere in ancient Maya sites, and scholars have demonstrated that the proportions of the ruined buildings, as well as the surface decoration, can be traced to its source in the scale patterns of the rattlesnake. They propose that the Classic Maya tuned in to cosmic order by observing the forms and patterns of reptiles, particularly the rattlesnake, and translated these cosmic proportions into their architecture.

The image of a grotesque mask forming the entrance to a magic place has become a standard feature in the design vocabulary of fantasy film. You may have seen this concept as part of the scenery in cartoons or children's TV shows.

Project 4–1: Sculpting a Mayan Mask Facade

PREPARATION

Gather pictures of Mayan buildings from the many books that are available on Mayan archaeology and tourism. Discuss the ceremonial function of the structures, and point out the animal imagery in relief sculpture decorating the walls and entrances. (See Figures 4–5 and 4–6.) Have students sketch the images that most appeal to them.

MATERIALS

- Sculptamold ™ (see note on following page) or plaster plaques, cast into a shallow box between 6 and 12 inches.
- pencils, paper
- tools: knives, nails, dental tools, wooden modeling tools, chopsticks
- stain made of diluted paint
- shellac or acrylic medium

Figure 4-5. A stack of masks carved in stone at Uxmal. (Photograph by Zebulon W. White.)

Figure 4-6. Stone mask frieze at Sayil, near Uxmal. (Photograph by Zebulon W. White.)

WORKING WITH SCULPTAMOLD

The material, in powder form, is a combination of paper pulp and plaster, available from school art supply catalogs, or art supply stores. Mix according to directions: add the dry Sculptamold™ to water—1 generous cup Sculptamold™ to 2/3 cup of water makes a fairly stiff paste. Spread in shallow boxes to make plaques for carving. Sculptamold™ sets up like plaster in about 20 minutes, but stays soft enough to impress with tools for a long period of time. Have students make an experimental piece to begin with, to learn how to handle the material and to become familiar enough with it to attempt a more developed relief sculpture.

PROCEDURE

1. Make flat plaques for relief sculpture as described above.
2. Let the material set. Then begin to work by pressing lines into the surface with a tool. Keeping tools moist while working helps keep the surface from shredding.
3. Develop the mask image with tools, gradually deepening the lines and delineating the form.
4. As you become familiar with the qualities of this material, you may want to add more dimension by building up the surface with fresh Sculptamold™. An experimental approach at the beginning stages will encourage confidence.
5. Sculptamold™ will harden very gradually over a period of weeks. (It can be baked for one hour at 200 degrees to harden, if desired.) When the pieces are hard enough, lightly stain with diluted paint and wipe, to look like old stone.
6. When the work is dry, it can be sealed with shellac or acrylic medium.

CONCLUSION

Have students arrange a display of their work, and talk about their experience of working with Sculptamold™. Evaluate the results. Figure 4–7 shows an actual studio art project.

FOLLOW-UP

Continue the study and creative interpretation of Maya architecture into three dimensions by having the students each use a small box, such as a shoe box or a cracker box, covered with Sculptamold™ to develop relief elements of decoration and embellishment. These pieces can then be displayed together as a model city.

CREATIVE WRITING

Discuss with the class the mystifying Maya abandonment of their great ceremonial centers. Write a hypothesis of why they may have just walked away from their cities some time in the tenth century.

Figure 4-7. Studio art project. Sculptamold™ was formed and carved into a mask/doorway on a corrugated cardboard support. (Artwork by Susan Hogan.)

MAYAN RELIEF SCULPTURE

For most of this century, archaeologists had been able to decipher only the highly complex and unique calendrical information given in the Mayan glyphs. In the 1970s and 1980s, scholars from universities in North America made tremendous breakthroughs in reading the entire meaning of this language carved in stone. They discovered that most of the figures and faces depicted in stone sculpture and on pottery vessels represent particular people—individual rulers and aristocrats intent on validating positions of power. The glyphs that surround their images describe the situations and events that they intended to commemorate.

Archaeologists figured out that the most potent and convincing ceremony in representing royal prestige was regular ritual bloodletting by the elite. The supplicant pierced himself or herself with a sharp instrument to let blood flow onto many pieces of paper, which were then burned in a bowl. Faces that emerge from glyphs for curls of smoke from these bowls suggest the appearance of the ancestor from the burning papers. The vision quest by bloodletting seems grotesque to us, but to the Maya, these hallucinations probably caused by loss of blood were passionate contact with the beings of the Otherworld. The regular visions legitimized their status in the social heirarchy.

Burning incense was a less spectacular mode of beckoning spirit beings. Incense burners are often personalized with sculptures of individuals who are engaged in just such a visionary quest.

Project 4–2: Making a Mayan Self-Portrait Pot

After molding each other's faces with Plastercraft®, students can use the face molds to form self-portraits in clay. When attached to a clay pot they construct for this purpose, their faces can be transformed into ancient Mayan characters by inventing Mayan hairdos, headdresses, and decorative surroundings with bits and pieces of clay. (See Figure 4–8.)

PREPARATION

Have students do design research for their project by gathering pictures of Mayan art and sculptures to use as visual reference material in developing Mayan-style clay ornamentation for themselves.

MATERIALS

- Plastercraft®, or gauze bandages coated with dry plaster, or Rigid Wrap®
- scissors
- bowls of water
- tissues
- newspapers
- white low-fire clay, cone 06
- electric kiln
- clay modeling tools
- terra cotta flowerpot

Figure 4-8. Ceramic censer from Guatemala, 5th-6th centuries, with a stylized seated figure emerging from a mask, and surrounded by abstract plant forms. (Courtesy of the Metropolitan Museum of Art, New York City. Gift of Carol R. Meyer, 1982.)

PROCEDURE

Part One: Making the Face Mold

1. To mold each others' face with Plastercraft®, work in pairs or groups of three. The first portrait subject sits tilted back, with his or her head resting on a table.

2. Before making the mask of Plastercraft®, place pieces of wet paper towel on the face to protect the subject's skin from plaster. Be sure to put wet towelling over the subject's eyes, as well.

3. Cut small strips of Plastercraft® so you will have a pile of them ready to use.

4. One by one, dip the Plastercraft® strips into the bowl of water and smooth onto the (damp paper towels over the) face.

5. Build up four layers of plaster strips to make sure the mask will be rigid enough.

6. Be sure the hairline is covered with wet toweling, as well as the ears. Apply plaster strips up to the hairline.

7. Work under the chin; leave nostrils open.

8. Let the plaster set up 5 minutes before removing; then trim the edges neatly.

9. When the plaster is cured, use the *inside* of each mold as a press-mold for the clay portrait.

10. Roll out a slab of clay, about 1/4-inch thick, and gently drape it over the inside of the plaster mask.

11. Work the clay carefully down into the concave forms of the face.

12. Make sure to add tabs to thicken and reinforce corners and places where there is stress, or thinning of the material.

13. Trim the edges of the clay mask neatly, making sure it is an even thickness.

14. Reinforce with moist clay where necessary.

15. Wrap the clay faces in plastic bags to keep them moist while you build the pot.

Part Two: Building the Pot for the Portrait Face

1. Using a terra cotta flowerpot or a similar form as an armature for support, cover it with newspaper so the pot will easily slip off the armature.

2. A relatively thick slab of clay will be needed to support the added weight of the clay face.

3. Form the clay around the mold, firmly joining the seam. The pot should be at least 8-inches high.

4. Trim the top edge.

5. When the clay is firm enough to stand without support, attach it to a bottom by setting it on a slab, and attaching it firmly with slip.

6. Unwrap the clay face, and let it stiffen enough to hold its form by sitting in warm, dry air.

7. The clay face will begin to shrink slightly away from the plaster. Then carefully work the clay out of its plaster form. It may need some touch-up and smoothing.

8. Place the portrait on the pot so that the top (forehead) extends above the rim about two inches. Use thick slip as "mortar," or glue, to hold it together.

9. The royal portraits are ready to be dressed in ornamental stones, feathers, and beads of clay. Refer to the Mayan sculptural resources for ideas to invent an elaborate personal style.

10. Freely add bits and balls and coils and twists of clay to develop the costume and jewelry, and don't forget the royal headdress to express prestige and power.

11. Remember that this special Mayan is emerging from surroundings of lush jungle—vines, roots, leaves, snakes—all to be expressed in stylized curlicues of clay.

12. As you cover the pot with coordinated motifs, make sure that the elements are all firmly "glued" on with slip.

13. To prevent warping and cracking, these creations should be dried slowly by covering them loosely with a plastic bag.

14. When bone dry, they can be stained with a commercial ceramic stain.

15. Bisque fire the dry pieces at cone 04. A second firing at cone 06 will bring the clay to its proper hardness.

CONCLUSION

Arrange the portrait pots for a class critique. Encourage the students to compare the appearance of their own portrait faces with the faces in Mayan sculpture. Figure 4–9 shows an actual studio art project.

Figure 4-9. Studio art project. A self-portrait in clay becomes an ancient Mayan personage on a jungle-inspired pot. (Artwork by Susan Hogan.)

FOLLOW-UP

Students can use their plaster face molds to create a series of more personal self-portraits.

CREATIVE WRITING

Discuss the issue of the self-induced hallucinations in Mayan rituals. Write an imaginary "trip" and speculate about the hallucinatory effect of bloodletting.

POLYCHROME CYLINDER VASES DEPICT
CLASSIC MAYAN MASKS AND ATTITUDES

Figure 4-10A. Seated figure in profile wears an animal mask and elaborate headdress. (Private collection.)

Figure 4-10B. A dialogue between a black monkey and a man in a black suit whose face emerges from the mouth of a mask. (Private collection.)

Figure 4-10C. Seated figure wears a crocodile mask and unique feathered headgear. (Private collection.)

Figure 4-10D. This red figure displays a feathered shield and sash in a procession of three similar figures. (Private collection.)

MAYAN CYLINDRICAL CLAY VESSELS

Cylindrical vases unearthed in archaeological excavations of ruined Mayan cities provide one of the clearest and most intricate records of their social customs and attitudes at the height of their culture. The detailed polychrome painting on these unique ceramics depicts particular lords and ladies, gods and goddesses in their ceremonies, processions, war victory parades, rituals, ball games, and festivals. (See Figures 4–10A through 4–10D.) They tell stories of the ruling elite's encounters with each other, and with the spirits of the Otherworld. Most of the figures are depicted in profile for graphic clarity in the linear mode of presentation. In sequential scenes like our cartoons, the figures sometimes speak in a stream of glyphs that issue from their mouths. Bordering glyphs record the specific date and occasion of the pictured scene.

The colors used are from earth pigments: the reds, oranges, and black are derived from iron compounds; the white and buff colors, from lime or clay. The vessels were fired in piles under burning stacks of wood. The quality of these small figure paintings on the vertical sides of cylinder pots reached a peak between 550 and 800 A.D. The most elaborate burials of the highest rulers often include many of such polychrome works. Most of these cylindrical jars have been extricated from tombs and are better preserved than ordinary household utensils or other art objects. They were significant, prized possessions that were apparently presented as gifts in homage to power by other elite personages. Some have been identified specifically as drinking vessels for cacao, or chocolate, the preferred beverage of the ruling classes.

A unique method of photographing these vases has been developed, called the rollout, in which a long horizontal photo shows the entire circular painting in one view. A rollout photograph is made by placing the vase on a rotating turntable, synchronized with a motorized camera. The resulting picture is a long band where all the painted images on the cylinder are visible together.

Project 4–3: Making a Painted Clay Cylinder Vase

PREPARATION

Ask the students to think of particular events in their lives that have been worth celebrating. Have them bring in photographs of a concert or party to use as subject matter to draw a scene of performance, music, dance, or celebration on their personal clay vessel. Use a photocopier to make enlarged copies of the photos, which can be used as stencils for drawing on the pots.

MATERIALS

- fat cardboard tubes such as salt cartons, oatmeal boxes, or sections of carpet roller to use as simple armatures for cylinders
- low-fire white clay, cone 06
- electric kiln
- basic clay modeling tools
- underglazes in three or four colors

PROCEDURE

1. Form a cylinder of clay around the cylindrical tube—about 8 inches tall—and even off the edges at the bottom and top.

2. Press out a slab of clay to fit the bottom. Use slip as glue, and attach the bottom to the cylinder. Trim to fit. Leave the top open.

3. When the clay is leather-hard, slowly and carefully remove the inner form.

4. The clay surface can be smoothed with a sponge.

5. Design a panorama of a party, music, or dance by using the photographs you have brought in.

6. Use a photocopier to multiply the figures and to modify the scale. Enlarge or shrink the photos on the copier to the correct scale for the cylinder pot.

7. Cut out the figures, place them on the pot, and trace around them with a pencil. You may have to keep cutting away more of each image to trace around the more interior parts of it.

8. Select a palette of three colors, and paint the figures with underglazes. You will understand why the Mayans depicted figures in profile: it is more dynamic, makes for a more interesting design, and conveys more information.

9. Make a decorative border, such as a musical theme, a staff, or notes, or a stylized song; on the top and around the bottom.

10. When all the pots are totally dry, fire them to cone 06.

11. If you think the visual images need more development after the bisque firing, add another level of drawing or painting with the underglazes.

12. Dilute satin clear transparent glaze with water—about 50 percent—and apply the glaze with a sponge. The clear glaze will appear opaque until it is fired.

13. Glaze fire the pottery to cone 06. (*Note*: Alternatively, the plain bisque-fired pot can be painted with acrylics and, of course, not fired a second time!)

CONCLUSION

Display the finished pieces together, and ask each student to describe the event pictured on his or her pot for the group. Figures 4–11A through 4–11D show an actual studio art project.

FOLLOW-UP

The students could continue to explore the possibilities of drawing and painting personal narratives on simple clay vessels.

CREATIVE WRITING

Write a proposal for funding an international touring exhibition of this group of ceramic art. In your writing, address the issues of cultural influences on art appreciation, and interpretation.

Figures 4-11A, 4-11B, 4-11C, and 4-11D. Studio art project. Lacking rollout photography facilities, this painting of a rock band on a clay cylinder is shown in four separate views. (Artwork by Susan Hogan.)

MAYAN FIGURINES FROM JAINA

Jaina is an island just off the west coast of Yucatan in the Gulf of Mexico that contains at least 20,000 burials, of which only 1,000 have been investigated. Thousands of small figurines of clay, that were originally buried with the dead, have been excavated. The small figures of people, different deities, or goddesses are lifelike in depicting particular, individual costumes and headdresses. (See Figures 4–12a and 4–12b.) These little ceramic artifacts have been a unique source of information about the customs of dress and social ranking in that long-gone era. Most are also musical instruments—rattles and simple flutes, called ocarinas.

Project 4–4: Making a Mayan Goddess Rattle

PREPARATION

Gather pictures or photocopies of several Jaina figurines from books on Mayan art and archaeology. These little clay pieces are specific characters dressed to represent social roles, and can stimulate a fresh approach to forming clay.

MATERIALS

- low-fire white clay, cone 06
- clay modeling tools
- wood boards to work on
- rolling pins or thick dowels to roll out small slabs
- cardboard tubes, such as paper toweling tubes, for armatures
- newspaper to cover the tubes
- electric kiln
- underglazes

PROCEDURE

1. Before constructing the figure, make the pellets for the rattle, so they will dry by the time they are needed to be placed inside the completed piece. Roll several little balls of clay for this purpose, and set them in a warm place to harden.
2. Cover each cardboard tube with newspaper so the complete sculptures will slip easily off the armature.
3. Press out a thin slab of clay, and form it over the cardboard tube.
4. Form shoulders and head at one end, using small patches of clay.
5. Leave the other end open temporarily in order to remove the armature later.
6. Sculpt a simple face.
7. Develop a costume on the figure by applying strips, rolls, and balls of clay.
8. Have fun inventing an elaborate headdress, varying your design from source figurines.
9. Close the bottom by using slip as "glue." Place the hollow figure on a thin slab, then trim it to fit.

Figures 4-12A and 4-12B. Clay figurines excavated from burials at Jaina, Campeche, are dressed in typical Classic Mayan attire. (Private collection.)

10. *Poke air holes* with a pin tool, using the holes as part of the costume ornament.

11. When the figure is complete, insert the dry clay pellets by making a small hole in the back of the figure.

12. Close the opening with a clay patch, and smooth.

13. When the rattles are dry, paint them with underglazes.

14. Bisque fire the work to cone 04.

15. Apply clear satin glaze, diluted 50 percent with water, for the second firing.

CONCLUSION

Display this group of clay figures together, and ask the students to offer verbal feedback to each other on the work. Figure 4–13 shows an actual studio art project.

Figure 4-13. Studio art project. This hollow clay rattle was inspired by a Mayan moon goddess figurine. (Artwork by Susan Hogan.)

FOLLOW-UP

- Students can sculpt a group of more personal and expressive figures in clay.

- **Portrait plate**: Large plates are a prevalent form of ceramic style found in Mayan archaeogical sites and dated between 400 and 800 A.D. They usually have an image of a person in profile, and carry glyphs or signs that tell about the person. Plates are a popular art form today, too. Many people collect plates, which are made to commemorate different events and famous people.

  Make a plate out of clay by pressing a thin slab into a paper plate, or a plaster press mold. Trim the edges carefully and allow it to dry. Then it will be ready to decorate.

  Using scissors as your tool, cut a profile drawing of a friend or family member. Or you can take turns posing with a partner in class. Trace around the profile in the center of the plate. Then add motifs (think of things that are signs of the person's interests and identity) in the space around the head, or design a border of repeating signs.

CREATIVE WRITING

Write an imaginary conversation among the little figure sculptures.

MAYAN WEAVING

Each Mayan village of Guatemala, and many in neighboring Mexico, expresses its identity with characteristic costume. Women weave and wear similar garments whose design has been established for centuries. Some Classic Maya sculpture depicts skirts and huipiles, or blouses, in the same style that is worn by Highland Maya women in Guatemala today. (See Figure 4–14.) Ixchel, goddess of weaving, appears in sculpture and painting of the Classic Maya, and

Figure 4-14. Mayan women weave at backstrap looms in central Guatemala. (Photograph by R. Clinton Taplin.)

her influence is still honored in the work of present-day women at their village looms. The backstrap loom still in use today can be seen depicted in the figurative ceramic arts that have been excavated at the ancient burial ground of Jaina. It is simply constructed of strips of wood, held in place by a strap around the weaver's back that allows the necessary tension to be placed on the weaving in progress. Women weave certain items and men work the larger, more complex looms that weave belts and serapes.

Contemporary Mayan women living in Guatemala and Mexico traditionally accept a clearly defined nurturing role as mother, wife, cook, and weaver. Women remain within the household to bear and raise children and tend to hearth and home, clothing, food, and housekeeping. Girls begin to help their mothers with women's work at a young age, when they take on care of younger siblings and begin to learn weaving on toy projects. Boys are allowed to play freely until they are taken to work with their fathers in the fields at about age 10. Thus, socialization into the expected gender role is early and seems to be completely polarized.

Mayan women continue to weave traditional clothing forms for their families. Although formerly all the yarn or thread was spun by hand from cotton or wool and dyed by hand with natural dyes from plants and insects, thread is now purchased and already dyed with synthetic dyes, including indigo. The signs and patterns woven into the cloth are intended to be a visible connection to the timeless world of the spirits and ancestors. A woman wearing her hand-woven huipil walks surrounded by woven emblems of her place in the cosmos, and the saints and symbols that bring rain, fertility, and growth. The brilliant designs in fabric, such as the men with a horse, the eight-pointed star and flower from antiquity, the trees of life and the plants, the turtle and deer, are kaleidoscopes of color full of meaning, that have been lovingly transmitted throughout the centuries. Wherever a woman goes, she remains the center of her hand-created mobile universe filled with harmony and renewal. (See Figure 4–15.)

All men in any particular Mayan village also wear garments of the same design, although some elements in their costume are adapted from the Spanish colonial-style clothing of their conquerors. There is great discrimination against Indians and against their traditional dress and identity. In the 1980s, this prejudice reached the level of ethnocide in western Guatemala. The highland Mayan men, in order to gain what they need from the larger society, and whose orbit extends further from domestic life, have recently tended to adopt ordinary shirt and pants in order to transcend the boundaries of class to access jobs and respect of the wider world.

Project 4–5: Weaving a Mat on a Cardboard Loom

Weaving on cardboard is a simple format that can be the basis for freedom of expression in fiber art.

PREPARATION

Have the students collect pictures of typical woven motifs from Central American textiles.

MATERIALS

- cardboard pieces cut from corrugated boxes, about 15" × 22" (can be larger or smaller depending on the time and resources you want to invest in this project)

Figure 4-15. A baby girl carried in a handwoven sling on her mother's back already wears a blouse that identifies her with her community. (Photograph courtesy of the Guatemalan Trade Commission.)

- rulers, pencils, scissors
- yarns of brilliant colors in a variety of textures and weights
- twine, string, ribbon
- large plastic yarn-weaving needles or tapestry needles

PROCEDURE

1. Mark even measurements of 1/8 inches along opposite ends of the cardboard.
2. Using scissors, cut a small V slot at each mark, along both ends.
3. Draw large simple motifs on the cardboard surface, where they will be placed in the mat. Darken the patterns with marker so they will be visible through the weaving.
4. To warp this cardboard loom, wind yarn around the notches, passing it back and forth across the surface.

5. Begin weaving either in the center or at one end of the loom by threading a strand of yarn in and out across the warp, pulling it through enough to continue for two or three more rows across.

6. Weave three or four more rows next to it with a contrasting color. Keep the weaving loose for an open texture that will go faster.

7. Continue to create stripes of different colors with different wefts.

8. As you become familiar with the process of weaving, begin to try weaving in different directions, such as diagonally.

9. Keep the weaving about 2 inches from the end of the warp, to leave a margin for fringe.

10. When the mats are completely woven (stopping 2 inches from each end) be sure that the final weft thread is woven very tightly, and fastened securely at the edge.

11. To needle weave or embroider the sketched motifs into their mats, students can select one color, and with the threaded yarn needle, draw freely to fill in the outline of the symbol, which should be visible through the loosely woven mat.

12. The side edges of the mat can be finished using a small crochet hook to twine the dangling extra yarn back along the edge.

CONCLUSION

Remove the completed weavings from the cardboard, and arrange a display, placing them all together on one wall. Figure 4–16 shows an actual studio art project.

FOLLOW-UP

Have students research myths about the origin and importance of weaving in Native American cultures.

CREATIVE WRITING

Use the word "weaving" as the beginning of free association and poetic speculation.

Vocabulary Worksheet for the Maya

Look up the following vocabulary words in a dictionary, write the definition, and then use the word in writing a sentence about the Maya. Use a separate sheet of paper for this activity.

armature	Jaina
backstrap	necropolis
bloodletting	Otherworld
cacao	opaque
calendrical	palette
censer	Plastercraft®
codex	polarized
conquistadores	quest
cosmos	rollout
cylindrical	sacbes
decimation	tributaries
glyphs	warp
hallucination	weft
huipil	Yucatan

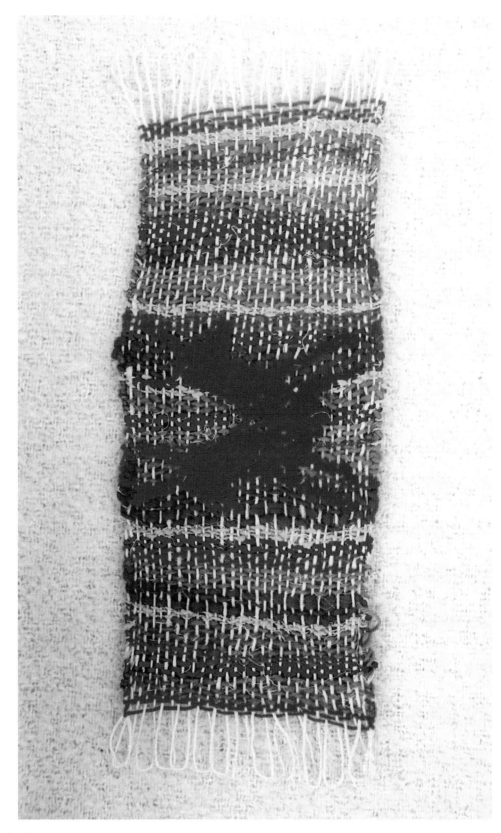

Figure 4-16. Studio art project. A two-headed deer symbol is drawn with thick red yarn and a blunt tapestry needle into the striped mat, which was loosely woven on a cardboard loom. (Artwork by Susan Hogan.)

Name _____ Date _____

Geography Worksheet for the Maya

Find the answers to these problems in world atlases and encyclopedias. Use the back of this sheet if you need more space.

- Remnants of the Classic Maya civilization have been excavated in what four countries? List all the ruins of ancient cities that you can find on the map of these countries.

  _____

  _____

- What river forms part of the border between Guatemala and Mexico? Find and name its tributaries, and describe its path to the Gulf of Mexico.

  _____

  _____

- What crop that was cultivated on the Pacific Slope of Guatemala was used for currency in the Classic Maya world? What crop is now grown there for export?

  _____

  _____

- Can you name six volcanoes of the Sierra Madre in the highland Maya region, and give their altitude in meters and in feet? Volcanic eruptions were the source of what material that was as important to the Maya as steel is to the industrial world?

  _____

  _____

- If you plan a cruise by ship around the Yucatan Peninsula, your route would coincide with the trading route of the large sea-going canoes of the Classic Maya, and with routes taken by some of the Spanish conquistadors. Describe your projected journey by water from the Laguna del Terminos in the west around to the Caribbean coast of Guatemala.

  _____

  _____

- Locate and describe some of the biospheres established in Maya territory in the Yucatan. Discuss the advantages to the world of preserving the tropical forest habitat.

  _____

  _____

Geography Worksheet for the Maya (continued)

- Locate the island of Jaina in the Gulf of Mexico. Why would this place have been selected as a burial place for all of the dead?

  _____

  _____

- Why was Cancun situated where it is? What geographical factors determine the suitability for a world-class resort?

  _____

  _____

Name _____ Date _____

Related Assignments for the Maya

1. **Art History**. Compare the art of the Maya with the sculpture and paintings of the Aztecs, analyzing similarities and significant differences.

2. **Language**. Read accounts of the long process of deciphering Mayan glyphs. Report on the most recent discoveries in this field.

3. **Current Events**. Follow the news of the conflict between the government and the indigenous Mayan people in western Guatemala. What are the issues? What are the implications of government oppression?

4. **Math**. Research the Mayan calendar and their 260-day cycle.

5. **Science**
   - *Radiocarbon dating in archaeological scholarship*: How was it developed, how does it work, and why is it used?
   - *Astronomy*: How did the Maya calculate the movements of the stars and planets? How did they apply astronomy in their lives?

6. **Costume Design**. Compare pictures of different Maya relief sculptures to study the elaborate costume components and their symbolism.

7. **Ecology**. What wildlife species survive in the jungles of the Mayan area? What is being done to protect them?

8. **Travelogue**. Gather travel brochures for resorts on the Caribbean Coast of the Yucatan and Belize. Plan a trip that will take you from present-day leisure far back in time.

9. **History**. Read about the Spanish colonization of the Yucatan and Guatemala.

10. **Literature**. Explore the mythic world of the Maya by reading excerpts from the *Popul Vuh* and *The Books of Chilam Balam*.

RESOURCES FOR TEACHING

BOOKS

Bertrand, Regis and Danielle Magne. *The Textiles of Guatemala*. London: Studio Editions (Liberty), 1991.

Fuerst, Ann H. (ed.). *Maya Art Activity Book*. San Diego: San Diego Museum of Man and San Diego Unified School District, 1994.

Oliphant, Margaret. *The Atlas of the Ancient World*. New York: Simon & Schuster, 1992.

Sexton, James D. (trans. and ed.). *Mayan Folktales; Folklore from Lake Atitlan, Guatemala*. New York: Anchor Books/Doubleday, 1992.

Turner, Wilson G. *Maya Designs*. New York: Dover, 1980.

VIDEOTAPE:

The Mysterious Maya, National Geographic Society, 1993. Phone: (800) 638-5405.

MUSEUM RESOURCES

Peabody Museum of Archaeology & Ethnology
Harvard University
11 Divinity Avenue
Cambridge, MA 02138
(617) 495-2248

San Diego Museum of Man
1350 El Prado, Balboa Park
San Diego, CA 92101
(619) 239-2001

PERIODICALS

Americas, published in English and Spanish six times a year by the Organization of American States, 19th Street and Constitution Avenue NW, Washington, D.C. 20006. Subscription information: 1-800-222-5405.

NATIONAL TOURIST OFFICE

Mexican Government Tourist Office
405 Park Avenue, Suite 1401
New York, NY 10022
(800) 446-3942; (212) 838-2949

BIBLIOGRAPHY

Albuquerque Museum. *Maya Treasures of an Ancient Civilization*. New York: Abrams, 1985.

Bertrand, Regis and Danielle Magne. *The Textiles of Guatemala*. London: Studio Editions (Liberty), 1991.

Bjerregaard, Lena. *Techniques of Guatemalan Weaving*. New York: Van Nostrand Reinhold, 1977.

Coe, Michael D. *The Maya* (5th ed.). London: Thames & Hudson, 1966-93.

Editors of Time-Life Books. *The Magnificent Maya*. Alexandria, VA: Time-Life Books, 1993.

Reents-Budet, Dorie. *Painting the Maya Universe: Royal Ceramics of the Classic Period*. Durham & London: Duke University Press, 1994.

Schele, Linda and David Freidel. *A Forest of Kings. The Untold Story of the Ancient Maya*. New York: William Morrow & Co., 1990.

Schele, Linda and Mary Ellen Miller. *The Blood of Kings. Dynasty and Ritual in Maya Art*. New York: George Braziller, Inc., 1986.

Stuart, George E. and Gene S. Stuart. *The Mysterious Maya*. Washington, D.C.: National Geographic Society, 1977.

Stuart, George E. and Gene S. Stuart. *Lost Kingdoms of the Maya*. Washington, D.C.: National Geographic Society, 1993.

Turner, Wilson G. *Maya Designs*. New York: Dover Publications, 1980.

Mali

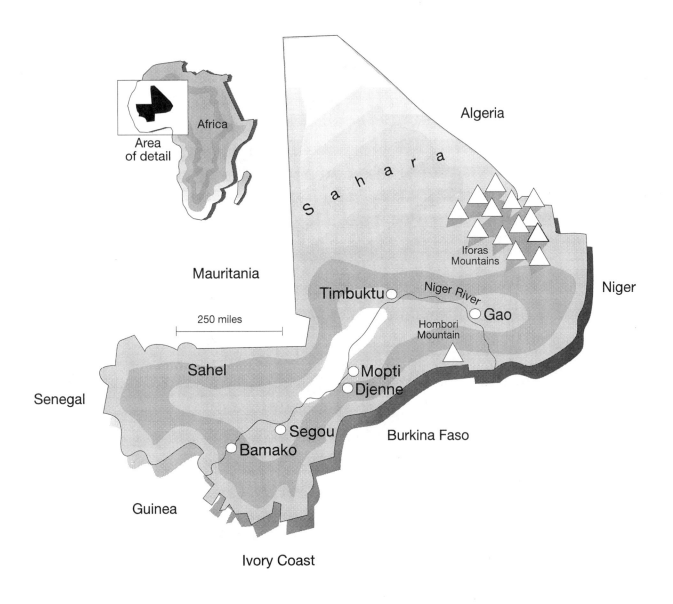

Area of detail

Africa

Algeria

Sahara

Mauritania

Iforas Mountains

Niger

Timbuktu

Niger River

Gao

Hombori Mountain

250 miles

Sahel

Mopti

Djenne

Senegal

Segou

Burkina Faso

Bamako

Guinea

Ivory Coast

A BRIEF HISTORY OF MALI

Mali, the West African nation (see Figure 5–1) that is now one of the five poorest countries in the world, was for many centuries the center of a wealthy empire. In the fifteenth century, it was the second richest imperial court in the world. Three celebrated empires flourished in this part of the Western Sudan between the eighth century to the seventeenth century:

- Empire of Ghana beginning in the eighth century
- Empire of Mali in the thirteenth century
- Empire of Songhai from the fifteenth to seventeenth centuries

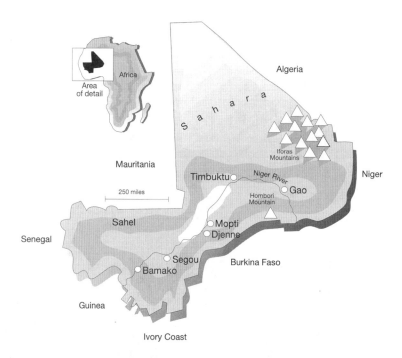

Figure 5-1. Map of Mali. This is a simplified locator map for quick reference. Students can look up a more detailed map of Mali in a world atlas.

Their power was founded on the wealth of the trans-Saharan trade, and the export of gold, slaves, ivory, and palm oil to the Mediterranean.

Gold mined in the west, near what is now Senegal, provided the prosperity to sustain the splendor of these gilded courts. One of Mali's legendary rulers, Mansa Musa, made a pilgrimage to Mecca in 1324. He lavished so much gold upon the inhabitants of Cairo enroute to Arabia that the local economy was almost completely undermined.

From this immense trans-Saharan journey, Mansa Musa brought back scholars who established a center of Islamic learning in Timbuktu. The cities of Mali had been founded on the Niger River as trading centers by the Moslems and they gradually became centers of scholarship and culture as well. The cities of Bamako, Djenne, Timbuktu, Segou, Mopti, and Gao were all built of mud, with distinctive mosque structures that are maintained with yearly mud plastering to this day.

The Sahara Desert covers 58 percent of Mali; the remaining terrain is the Sahel, or "Shore" of the great desert, the Niger delta, and the savannah, or grasslands that extend to the forest of the south. The Niger River, the great waterway of Mali, flows east from its origin in the hills of Senegal, spreads into a great 'bend' through Mali, and flows south through the countries of Niger and Nigeria into the Atlantic Ocean. The central area of savannah has been undergoing desertification in the past few decades; since the drought that began in 1968, rainfall has been slowly but steadily diminishing, and forcing difficult life changes on these African peoples.

Arab slave traders transported slaves from West Africa up through the Sahara until the 1600s, when Europeans began to ship human cargo from the Atlantic coast to the Americas, a practice that continued well into the nineteenth century. Most African slaves brought to the Americas were taken from homelands in West Africa. In the late 1800s, France claimed much of West Africa as its own and imposed national boundaries across the vast desert and savannah. This part of French West Africa became the independent nation of Mali in 1960. Soviet advisors stepped in and attempted to set up national socialism. After most of these government enterprises failed, Africans took control of their own nation in the 1980s.

Although most of the distinct ethnic groups of Mali, including the Malinke, Songhai, Fulani, Tuareg, Bozo, Bambara, and even the Dogon have been converted from their original religion of *animism* to Islam, they have managed to maintain community traditions that express their cultural identity. Continual foreign influence and government exploitation, cultural destruction by outsiders, and "modernization" have not yet eradicated the distinctive lifestyles of the peoples of Mali. Their communities have been somewhat protected by the harsh, inhospitable terrain, extreme heat, and insects as well as the lack of modern roads, plumbing, or comfortable facilities for visitors.

Project 5–1: Map Painting

This is a visual research assignment that will gradually provide abundant material for a collage painting of the country. Begin this project first, and finish it last, after students have completed the other studio projects and research. Have students record their information on the map(s); when they have done the rest of the projects, come back to this as a final expression of their journey through Mali. (See Figure 5–2 for an actual studio art project.)

Make several copies of the map of Mali to keep a visual record of research as it unfolds. As students find out more and more facts about Mali, have them:

- Write notes on the map.
- Locate the cities on the Niger River, find pictures of them to photocopy, and attach them with a glue stick.
- Locate the domains of the different peoples; indicate terrain, environment, climate, weather, products, arts and crafts, distinctive architecture, and design motifs.
- Include collage sketches, photos from travel brochures, and photocopies of pictures from books on Mali.
- Add historical notes, textures, and tour itineraries, filling up as many maps with information and material as needed.

When the class is near completion of the study of Mali, students can select the most compelling images from their visual map notes to use in a collage painting. Instructions for completing the map collage painting are given at the end of this chapter.

THE BAMBARA PEOPLE OF CENTRAL MALI

The Bambara are sedentary people who farm as a way of life. They are the dominant group in the central area, in and around the capital city of Bamako, and the city of Segou on the Niger. In addition to French, the Bambara language is the functional language of trade, commerce, and government bureaucracy in Mali.

The chi wara is a great symbol of motivation for Bambara farmers. Chi wara means lion of work; it is at the center of the yearly ritual to celebrate hard work and greater production. The antelope headdresses (see Figure 5–3 on page 153), carved of wood, are worn in a dance to celebrate farming, which requires very intense hard work between May and October each year. The dances are customarily performed before the rain and after the harvest, including the entire community in their scope and energy.

The male antelope mask, or crest, has a carved ornamental mane; the female carries the baby on her back. They are sculpted by artisans who are born into the artisan wood-carver caste. The skill and knowledge of the form, content, and material is passed down from father to son. The family initiates the youth into knowledge of the culture, which they embody in their traditional sculpture. The entire community relies on the artisan's knowledge and his integrity and commitment to his craft. Both male and female chi waras are worn by male dancers in this ritual.

Look at the elegant silhouettes of these archaic chi wara forms. (See Figures 5–4A and 5–4B.) They are inspired by the graceful flowing forms of the antelope head and horns. The designs are an abstract organic shape. The thin tapered forms seem to grow, flow, move in space, and define it. Study the graceful relation of "positive" form to "negative" space in these shapes.

Project 5–2: Chi Wara Carving

PREPARATION

For this project, you will use styrofoam instead of the traditional African wood because it is lighter and much easier to carve. In the U.S., compressed styrofoam (not the coarse granular type) is customarily used to carve props and set pieces for theatre and film. Masks and head-dresses for such festivals as Mardi Gras and other parades are usually made out of this type of styrofoam. It is easy to cut and very flaky, so use a large sheet or dropcloth under and all around students' workspace to catch all the flyaway chips; it will make cleanup a lot easier. Have students try cutting and chipping a small piece of styrofoam to first explore the material before they cut into a larger design.

MATERIALS

- paper and pencil
- insulation (blue or pink) styrofoam (can be purchased at hardware or building supply stores)

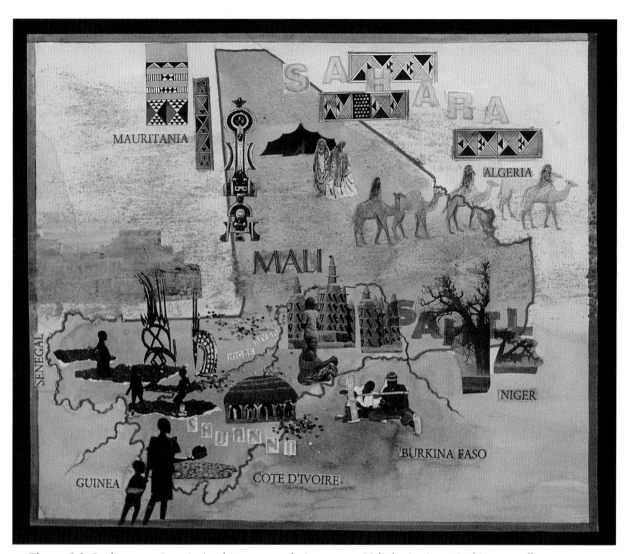

Figure 5-2. Studio art project. A visual journey exploring remote Mali destinations via this map collage. (Artwork by Susan Hogan.)

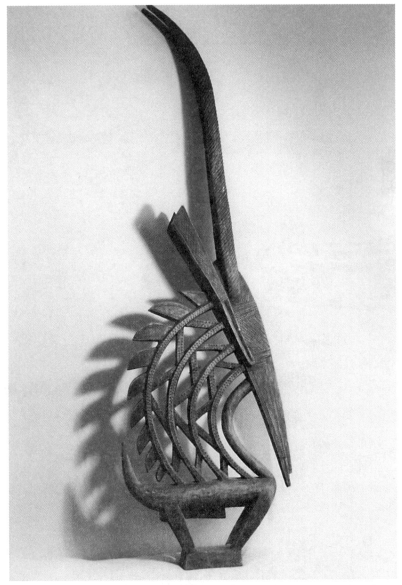

Figure 5-3. Bambara chi wara from Mali carved out of wood has an intricate mane, finely incised detail, and decorative brass studs. (Courtesy of Mana Diakite.)

- ballpoint pen
- small 5-inch finely serrated kitchen knife
- scissors
- utility knife
- rasp or Surform®
- gesso and brush
- tape
- thin paint for stain
- shellac or varnish

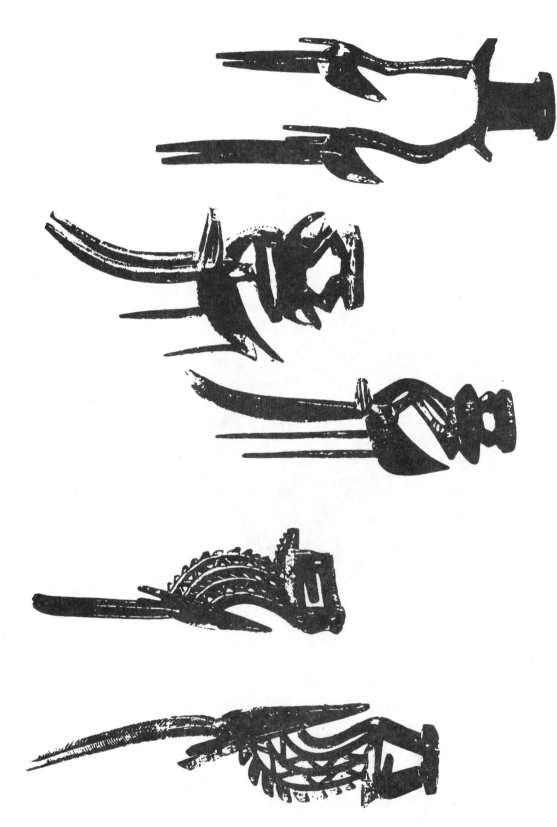

Figure 5-4A. Chi wara forms.

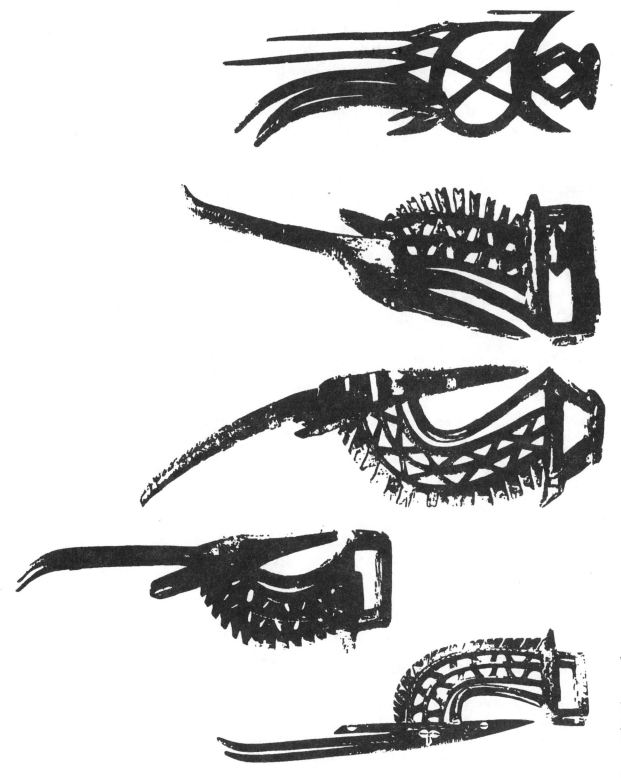

Figure 5-4B. Chi wara forms.

PROCEDURE

1. Study the shapes of the chi waras in Figures 5–4A and 5–4B.
2. Look up photos of chi waras in books on African sculpture.
3. Design an abstract organic shape on paper.
4. Make several thumbnail sketches to try your own variations on this theme.
5. Select your favorite sketch to draw in 1/2 scale.
6. Cut out the silhouette. Then continue to refine it by paring it down with scissors, balancing and streamlining the shapes within the design.
7. Enlarge your design to full scale and place it on top of the styrofoam.
8. Tape it in place.
9. Gently impress the lines with a ballpoint pen to indent into the styrofoam.
10. Remove the paper pattern.
11. Cut out the shape, using a gentle sawing motion with the serrated knife.
12. Round off the form by gradually carving down the edges and corners.
13. Paint with gesso (two coats).
14. Stain with thin earth-toned (tempera or acrylic) paint.
15. Shellac or varnish with matte medium.

Figure 5–5 shows an actual studio art project.

CONCLUSION

- Compare your rough-hewn chi wara with the carefully smoothed and finished sculpture crafted by a Bambara artisan.
- When you tie this "crest" to the top of your head, how does it feel? Do you feel connected to this mythical animal?

FOLLOW-UP

Take photos of the class in their new chi wara headdresses.

CREATIVE WRITING

Taking the point of view of a Bambara woman, explain to an outsider why the men performers wear the chi wara crests at the harvest dance.

THE TUAREG PEOPLE OF THE NORTHERN DESERT

Tuareg are desert nomads who have traditionally lived in the northern part of Mali that is the Sahara. These "blue men of the desert" (from the indigo dye of the blue veils they wear that represent wealth) are descended from the Berber people who fled into the desert centuries ago to escape the Arab invasion of their land in North Africa. Now they inhabit the Sahel, or "shore" of the Sahara, in northern Mali. They are nomads who move their herds of sheep,

Figure 5-5. Studio art project. This simplified chi wara form carved out of Styrofoam, then painted with gesso and acrylic paint, could almost pass for the real thing. (Artwork by Susan Hogan.)

goats, and camels from one sparse grazing area to another, following the available grass in the desert. For centuries these desert dwellers have roamed across several countries; now the governments want to force them to stay in one place. The Tuaregs have developed a distinctive lifestyle adapting to their harsh desert environment by breeding camels for the trans-saharan trade caravans. Now in the late twentieth century, their traditional way of life is more and more threatened by severe drought and the consequent loss of their herds to starvation, and by political conflict over national boundaries.

Tuareg *smiths*, or craftsmen, are a distinctive caste who make all the articles of daily use. A caste that is treated as a race apart, they also practice medicine and veterinary care. Both the men, known as *inadan*, and the women (*tinaden*) work leather in geometric designs from Islamic influence. Designs are traditionally geometric, strong and simple motifs that express the austerity and clear focus of their life in a hostile land where there are few organic, growing forms to inspire them. Their designs are based on constellations of stars by which they navigate in the desert, and the four cardinal directions. Triangles and magic squares have a talismanic function as well—protections from the "evil eye." (See Figures 5–6A and 5–6B.)

Tuareg smiths handcraft items for personal and tribal use from the raw materials they produce themselves, particularly leather from their animals. The wives tan and dye the leather and sew leather goods, including amulet boxes for men and woven leather bracelets for

Figures 5-6A and 5-6B. Tuareg embroidered pillow covers show quadrants of the four directions. (Courtesy of Mana Diakite.)

women. The men make the camel saddles, saddle bags, and water bags, as well as work in metal. Tuareg crosses are made of silver, the metal "blessed by the Prophet." (Gold is traditionally the metal of the devil.) In recent years, the Tuareg have been desperate for cash to enable them to survive, so they've been selling their craftwork to tourists, traders, or whoever will pay money for the distinctive tooled cases, belts, bags, and scabbards.

Project 5–3: Making a Tuareg-style Leather Bag

PREPARATION

Gather design resources from source books on the Tuareg, or use the design resource given in Figure 5–7.

MATERIALS

- paper, rulers, and chalk or pencil
- scissors
- thin leather
- yarn in brilliant colors for tassles and fringe
- gel medium or white glue
- acrylic or fabric paints in three or four colors
- clothespins for clamps

PROCEDURE

1. Cut a rectangle of leather 24 inches long and 10 inches wide.
2. Fold the long piece into a bag 9 inches deep, leaving a 6-inch flap.
3. With the better side of the leather inside, glue along 1/4 inch of the side seams, and clamp with clothespins until set.
4. Using pencils and rulers, design bands of triangle motifs on paper as a pattern of painted decoration for the bag.
5. Still waiting for the glued side seams to dry, make 5 or 6 long colorful tassles out of the yarn by wrapping about 8 inches of yarn 12 times (the width of a school notebook will give you about the correct length).
6. Finish the tassles by binding the tops with contrasting yarn.
7. Braid a handle from three colors; use 40-inch strands of yarn.
8. When the side seams are dry enough to hold, turn the bag right-side out.
9. Referring to your pencil design, draw the bands of triangle motifs onto the leather, using a ruler and chalk or pencil.
10. Use acrylic or fabric paint to paint the motifs on the surface.
11. Glue the tassles onto the bottom of the bag, and onto the flap.
12. Attach your braided handle.
13. Finish off with more cutouts, appliqué, fringe, or beads if you wish. (See Figures 5–8A and 5–8B.)

Figure 5-7. Detail of a Tuareg saddle bag with leather and cotton appliqués, painted, incised, and peeled motifs. (Reprinted from *African Nomad Designs* by permission of Dover Publications.)

Figure 5-8A. Large Tuareg leather bag for carrying necessities of nomadic life, decorated with long fringe and triangular cutouts. (Courtesy of Mana Diakite.)

Figure 5-8B. The reverse side of Tuareg bag. (Courtesy of Mana Diakite.)

CONCLUSION

Display the completed bags as a group, affirming the creative challenge of adapting tribal traditions to classroom art. To pursue the process of designing leather bags, use a photo collage. The class can invent a storeload of creative bags: have them cut out fashion photos of handbags to paint with patterns and/or collage with photo elements (jewelry, flowers, etc.). See Figure 5–9 for an actual studio art project.

FOLLOW-UP

Have the class research the lifestyle of desert nomads in the Western Sudan today, and report on the current situation of these peoples.

CREATIVE WRITING

Imagine what it would be like to live in the deep Sahara, to make regular travels across the dunes on camelback, and to constantly set up new temporary settlements with your tribe. Remember the desert environment of starry sky and vast stretches of empty terrain. Write about living in that situation.

THE FULANI PEOPLE OF THE NIGER DELTA

Fulani people are also nomadic pastoralists who have traditionally grazed their herds across the savannah, or grasslands south of the desert. Several different groups of Fulani people inhabit the Niger delta. They have traditionally lived on the products of their immense herds of cattle. In recent years, they have been forced to settle by the drought and by changes in government land policies. In the partly settled Fulani communities, the younger sons of the household move with the herds. During the dry season, the delta, or floodplain, of the Niger River is the only place in the country where green fodder for livestock can be found.

Fulani communities have adapted to changing conditions by embracing a wide range of new lifestyles. Still, they are held together by a common background. The most important things to them are family, cattle, personal appearance, and skill at dancing and poetry.

The more settled Fulani have developed a materialistic, heirarchical society in which they express their status by wearing elaborate ornamental hairstyles and jewelry. Near the city of Djenne on the Niger, a skullcap of amber beads is worn by single young women. Once they are married, they exchange the skullcap of beads for enormous gold earrings. The gold is a sign of wealth and value in social standing. Beads are also worn as a demonstration of wealth and identity, as well as for protection against outside harm. Different beads have specific healing functions.

Hair is sculptural material for artistic expression. It is dressed with oil, shaped over padding, and adorned with an assortment of beads that denote regional differences of identity, age, and social standing. Songhai women in Timbuktu and Gao still wear elaborate *coiffures* that show influences from the Songhai Empire of 500 years ago. European coins originally introduced as currency are now widely used as hair decorations, and melted down coinage is used to make silver bracelets, hair rings, and repoussé beads.

Beads have a long history in African trade. (See Figure 5–10.) When the Europeans first began their African trade, they quickly discovered how much the Africans liked glass beads, so they ordered shiploads of beads made in Venice, Italy, to offer the Africans in exchange for trade goods. The Africans themselves began making beads out of glass, by using the whiskey bottles and cosmetic jars left by the Europeans. They crushed this glass, then poured it into ceramic molds, and baked the molded beads in an earthen oven. The glass fused, but did not melt, thus the sandy texture of these African glass beads.

For centuries, cowry shells from the Indian Ocean had been used as currency and applied to hats, clothing, and furniture. They were drilled and used as components in jewelry, as were clam shells from the Atlantic, ivory, small bones, amber, and semi-precious stones.

Figure 5-9. Studio art project. This leather bag is constructed from thrift-shop leather, painted with decorative triangle bands in Tuareg colors of red and green. Braided handle and tassles are made of multi-color yarn. (Artwork by Susan Hogan and Ruth Neustadter.)

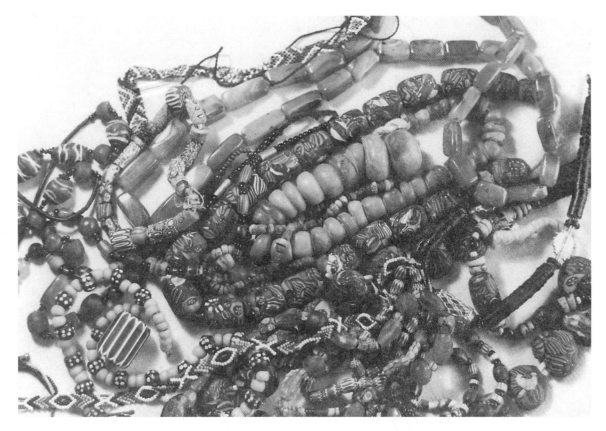

Figure 5-10. African trade beads can be seen in any West African market. (Courtesy of Mana Diakite.)

Gold and silver were worked into fine filigree pendants or repoussé beads. Invention and imagination in ornamentation were exuberant and elaborate.

African jewelry changes according to materials available, cultural contacts, and terrain inhabited by the group. Each group practices unique ceremonies and rituals. Different and complex beliefs engender a wonderful variety of forms in symbolic jewelry, which expresses a way of relating to each other and to the world. (See Figure 5–11.)

Project 5–4: Making African Trade Beads of Polymer Clay

PREPARATION

Before students begin to make African-inspired beads and jewelry, encourage them to visit African import stores and museums to study existing styles and uses. They can gather ideas and inspiration from the juxtaposition of abundant "stuff."

MATERIALS

- package of multicolor polymer clay
- brown paper to cover work surface

- wire to string soft beads
- foil-covered baking pan
- oven set at 275° (or manufacturer's instructions)
- gloss varnish spray

PROCEDURE

1. Start by selecting two colors of polymer clay to combine.
2. Cut a small section off each block of color.
3. On your work surface, roll each color out into a thin coil.
4. Then twist the two colors together, creating a striped spiral roll.
5. Cut the spiral clay roll into short sections.
6. Roll these sections into rounded beads.
7. String the soft beads onto a piece of wire for baking.
8. Place your first batch onto the foil-covered baking pan.
9. Now, try three different colors together.
10. Twist the three colors together.
11. Then fold over and twist again, creating a marbled effect.
12. Cut your marbled clay roll into bigger sections.
13. Shape the marbled sections into large oval beads.
14. String onto wire for baking.
15. Now invent your own combinations.
16. Make enough matching beads to use together when you combine them with others in necklaces.
17. Bake your tray of polymer beads in an oven set at 275° for about 45 to 50 minutes.
18. Keep an eye on the baking beads to make sure they don't brown.
19. Remove beads from the oven, and set aside to cool and harden.
20. First varnish one side by spraying with a gloss varnish.
21. Let dry, then turn the beads over and spray the other side.
22. Ready to string, but wait. . . . See Project 5–5.

Project 5–5: Stringing African-inspired Necklaces

PREPARATION

How many materials can you make beads from? Collect old jewelry, organic forms from nature, twisted wire . . . be inventive.

MATERIALS

- baked polymer beads
- shells, twigs, coins, wire, old jewelry, seeds, etc.

Figure 5-11. African trade beads. (Courtesy of Mana Diakite.)

- a small drill such as a Dremel tool
- heavy-duty upholstery thread, or raffia

PROCEDURE

1. Drill small holes into your collected materials.
2. Lay out an arrangement of beads.
3. Try different combinations of polymer beads with old beads, shells, coins, wood, etc.
4. String them onto heavy-duty thread. See Figure 5–12 for an actual studio art project.

Figure 5-12. Studio art project. Beads of marbled polymer clay are strung with twigs, shell, mica, and coins. (Artwork by Susan Hogan, Anique Taylor, and Virginia Cornne.)

CONCLUSION

Students can model their creations in an impromptu fashion show.

FOLLOW-UP

Have the class arrange a merchandising display of their African-inspired jewelry on a background of natural materials such as sand, pebbles, wood, or stones.

CREATIVE WRITING

Work in small groups to write an imaginative presentation for selling your jewelry on a TV shopping network.

THE DOGON PEOPLE OF THE BANDIAGARA CLIFFS IN SOUTHEAST MALI

The Dogon people retreated to the harsh terrain of the cliffs of the Bandiagara Escarpment during the fifteenth century to protect themselves from pressure to convert to Islam. There was no soil in this rocky land, until they collected soil from the Niger Delta and transported it bag by bag to their settlements. They built rock terraces and walls to create small plots for agriculture. They have evolved community customs that support their lifestyle in harmony with the land here, and still cultivate millet, maize, rice, tomatoes, onions, and other vegetables. They also keep a few goats and sheep.

There are close to 700 Dogon villages within several square miles along the barren rocky cliffs, where the people have developed architecture and town planning totally unique in appearance and completely symbolic of their mythic relationship to the universe. Each of these villages is laid out as a human body, as is each dwelling, with a head, belly, arms and hands, and legs and feet. Maintaining the survival of the villages has required close adherence to powerful traditions of hard work, social relationships, and community identity.

Men's societies have evolved to maintain their tribal unity and their connection from generation to generation. Men, who gather in the men's huts that are forbidden to women to enter, guard the secrets of their conferences from inquisitive intruders. They practice an oral story tradition, passing along their heritage—symbolic relation of individual to family, tribe, place, and cosmos. The powerful alliance with ancestors in their rituals and art has made it possible for the Dogon to continue to resist outside religious influence for centuries, specifically Islam.

Eight mythical ancestor figures appear in Dogon ritual woodcarving, teaching the stories of their cosmic origin and identity in a tangible, visible form. The sculptors are smiths who are born into the artisan trade, into the duty and privilege of making the ritual art out of wood and iron, including doors, posts, masks and stilts for dances, and other devotional sculpture. (See Figures 5–13A, 5–13B, and 5–13C.) Figures are carved as tangible prayers for rain, fertility, and protection from evil. The rows of eight primal ancestor figures carved on doors are believed to confer power and energy on their descendents. Posts of men's society huts are carved with power figures for protection and authority.

These traditional Dogon doors (see Figure 5–14) and posts have become so valued in the art markets of the West that they have all but disappeared from the villages. The people can

Figures 5-13A, 5-13B, and 5-13C. Dogon masks carved of wood in powerful forms that reflect the strong light of Africa. (Courtesy of African Art Museum, Tenafly, New Jersey.)

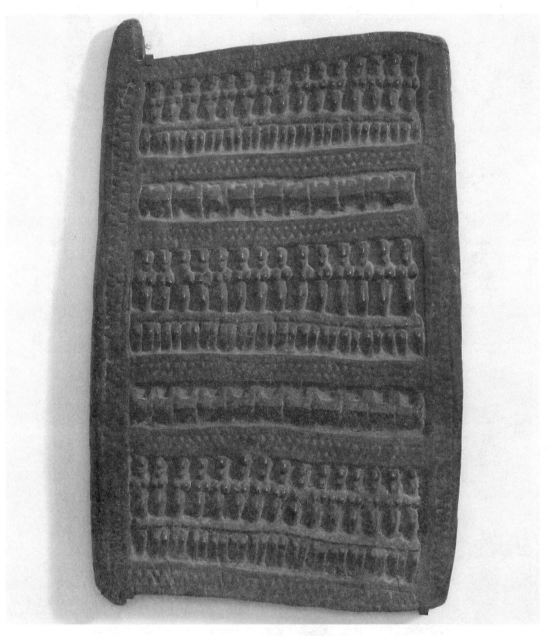

Figure 5-14. This distinctive Dogon carved granary door has rows of stylized figures alternating with rows of frogs and zigzag lines representing water, or speech. (Private collection.)

get so much money for their artifacts that they can't resist selling them, or they hide the work away from the eyes of foreign traders. The unique sculptures that transmit the ancient Dogon world-view and ideals of life in visible form have been sold and dispersed in art markets and auction houses in the Western cities. The disappearance of these totems of tribal identity is, of course, a factor in the gradual dissolution of their rigorously committed way of life.

The Dogon villages have been named a World Heritage Site, and laws have been passed to protect their work from being totally removed from its proper home and function. Only time will tell if these measures will be effective in helping to preserve the integrity of the culture.

Project 5–6: Dogon Woodcarving Project

PREPARATION

Inspired by Dogon sculpture, approach carving in wood as a way to reflect upon your ancestors, the people who came before you. A good image to use might be a myriad of faces, or a tree growing into many branches. Consider the way the Dogon make optimum use of every resource in their harsh environment. Wood is a precious material because very few trees grow near the Bandiagara Cliffs, so it is treated with respect.

MATERIALS

- take a trip to gather wood—driftwood, logs from the woods, small scraps of plywood or soft pine boards (can be collected from construction sites); thick bark from fallen trees is very good for carving easily; pieces of wood approximately 12 inches in length and width should be about the right size for this project
- linoleum cutting tools
- pen knives, Swiss Army knives, or small kitchen knives
- shellac or acrylic medium and brushes

PROCEDURE

1. Make a preliminary "test" piece of carving with the tools to learn how different pressures, marks, and directions will work on the wood. Start gently and carefully, becoming comfortable with the carving process.
2. Think of tree energy—growing upward and branching (an appropriate metaphor for the family tree). Or think of a myriad of faces beginning to peer out of the material, at first very elemental, then gradually developing into distinct visages.
3. Develop your wood pieces by gradually deepening and extending the wood-cutting marks.
4. When carvings are complete, seal the wood with shellac or acrylic medium.

CONCLUSION

Arrange a display of the wood carvings. Figure 5–15 shows an actual studio art project.

FOLLOW-UP

Encourage the class to discuss the world market for tribal art. Why would outsiders be so eager to own the primitive art of the Dogon people?

CREATIVE WRITING

Imagine you are a dealer in tribal art who is traveling to Mali to purchase artwork to sell in a gallery. What would you look for and how would you approach artisans? Write an imaginary dialogue between yourself and the art maker.

Project 5–7: Mali Map Collage Painting

PREPARATION

Now students will have the opportunity to use the Mali maps they have been filling with cultural and geographical images and information. (Refer to Project 5–1.)

MATERIALS

- 24" by 30" or larger heavyweight paper
- glue sticks
- photos, photocopies
- sand, beads, African fabric (should be available in fabric stores)
- white glue
- crayons or watercolor crayons
- cutouts to use as stencils
- watercolor paints and brushes
- containers for water

PROCEDURE

1. Sketch the map outline onto heavyweight paper, 24" by 30" or larger.
2. Add collage elements with your glue stick—food in the markets, boats on the Niger, photos of the mud mosques, etc.
3. Use cutouts as stencils; for example, you could use a camel cutout to trace around to draw a caravan from Timbuktu to the eastern boundary of Mali and beyond.
4. Add words to label the different regions: Sahara, Sahel, Bandiagara, the cities, the river, the peoples.
5. Add texture: sand (mixed with diluted white glue augments the desert areas), or fabric, or beads.
6. Keep building up the picture with words, images, and textures.
7. Use watercolor paints to develop the picture into a fully resolved painting.

CONCLUSION

Arrange a display of the map collages, and then have each student describe his or her own map interpretation to the class.

FOLLOW-UP

Ask the students where they would choose to go as Peace Corps volunteers in Mali. What would they choose to contribute to that community?

CREATIVE WRITING

Write a film script for a travel video through Mali.

Figure 5-15. Studio art project. A myriad of faces carved easily into thick bark with a penknife and lino-cutting tools evoke family lineage. (Artwork by Susan Hogan.)

Name _____   Date _____

Vocabulary Worksheet for Mali

Look up the definition of each of these words in a dictionary and then use the word in writing a sentence about Mali. Use a separate sheet of paper for this activity.

animism	indigo
artifacts	integrity
artisan	mosque
caravans	mythical
caste	nomads
chi wara	pastoralist
coiffures	rigorously
crest	savannah
desertification	sedentary
dissolution	skullcap
evil eye	smiths
exploitation	talismans
filigree	thumbnail sketches
fodder	totems
heirarchical	trans-Saharan trade
herders	

Geography Worksheet for Mali

Refer to world atlases and travel guides to answer these problems. If you need more space, use the back of this sheet.

- Look at the extent of the Sahara Desert in Africa, and describe the rate at which the desert is expanding.

  _____

  _____

- Describe the area known as the Sahel, and write about how different peoples adapt to living in this geographic zone.

  _____

  _____

- Locate the Bandiagara Plateau on a topographical map and describe the geographical features that have made this area a relatively protected habitat for the Dogon.

  _____

  _____

- Describe the path of the Niger River as it makes its way from Senegal to the Atlantic Ocean.

  _____

  _____

- Identify the cities located along the Niger River. Describe their physical attributes, economies, and populations.

  _____

  _____

Geography Worksheet for Mali (continued)

- Describe the way seasonal changes in weather affect the people who inhabit the towns and villages of the Niger Delta.

  _____

  _____

- Define desertification and explain how it is affecting the lives of all the peoples of Mali.

  _____

  _____

Related Assignments for Mali

1. **History**. Research the slave trade in West Africa. Locate the population centers that were most affected by it, and describe the transition of culture from Africa to the New World.

2. **Archaeology**. Look up the excavation sites in Mali where terra cotta and bronze antiquities are being dug up and sold to the international art market. What cultural records are being dispersed forever in this way? Why are laws of cultural preservation ineffective?

3. **Architecture**.
   - Mosques in the various cities
   - *Dogon architecture*
   - *Tents of the Tuareg herders*
   - *Muslim* artistic influence in building

4. **Travelogue**. Have students plan a trip through Mali with a particular focus, using travel books and articles as a resource of information and ideas.

5. **Costume studies**. Make sketches of the different styles of dress. Use brilliant fabrics, brilliant colors, and prints. Consider the way costume and jewelry are worn as symbols of status and identity.

6. **Biography**
   - Ibn Battuta
   - Mansa Musa

7. **Topics for further research**
   - musical instruments
   - dances

RESOURCES FOR TEACHING

BOOKS

Dostert, Pierre Etienne, J. D. *Africa 1996*. Harper's Ferry, WV: Stryker-Post Publications, The World Today Series, revised annually.

Freeman-Grenville, G. S. P. *The New Atlas of African History*. New York: Simon & Schuster, 1991.

Murray, Jocelyn (ed.). *Cultural Atlas of Africa*. New York: Facts on File Publications, 1981.

Prussin, Labelle. *African Nomadic Architecture: Space, Place, & Gender*. Washington, D.C.: Smithsonian, 1995.

VIDEOTAPE

"*Art of the Dogon*," Metropolitan Museum of Art, New York.

PERIODICALS

African Arts, published quarterly by UCLA, J. S. Coleman African Studies Center, UCLA, Los Angeles, CA 90095-1310.

Ornament, published quarterly by Ornament Inc., P.O. Box 2349, San Marcos, CA 92079-2349. Phone: (619) 599-0228.

MUSEUM RESOURCES

The African Art Museum of the SMA Fathers
23 Bliss Avenue
Tenafly, NJ 07670
(201) 567-0450

National Museum of African Art
Smithsonian Institution
950 Independence Avenue, S.W.
Washington, D.C. 20560
(202) 357-4600

BIBLIOGRAPHY

African Arts, Autumn 1995, Vol. XXVIII, No. 4. "Protecting Mali's Cultural Heritage."

Atmore, Anthony and Gillian Stacey. *Black Kingdoms, Black Peoples*. London: Orbis, 1979.

Attenborough, David. *The Tribal Eye*. New York: W.W. Norton, 1976.

Courtney-Clarke, M. *African Canvas*. New York: Rizzoli, 1990.

Davidson, Basil. *African Civilization Revisited*. Trenton, NJ: Africa World Press, 1991.

The deHavenon Collection, Museum of African Art, Washington, D.C., 1971.

Fisher, Angela. *Africa Adorned*. New York: Harry N. Abrams, 1984.

Gordon, Albert F. and Leonard Kahan. *The Tribal Bead. A Handbook of African Trade Beads*. New York: Tribal Arts Gallery, Inc., 1976.

Halliburton, Warren J. *Nomads of the Sahara*. New York: Crestwood House (Macmillan), 1992.

Horn, Diana Victoria. *African Nomad Designs*. Owings Mills, MD: Stemmer House, 1992.

Koslow, Philip. *Centuries of Greatness. The West African Kingdoms, 750-1900*. New York: Chelsea House Publishers, 1995.

Middleton, John (ed.). *Peoples of Africa*. New York: Arco, 1978.

Moody, Jo. *The Book of Jewelry*. New York: Simon & Schuster, 1994.

Newton, Alex. *West Africa*. (A Lonely Planet travel survival kit.) Hawthorne, Australia: Lonely Planet Publications, 1988.

O'Toole, Thomas. *Mali . . . in Pictures*. Minneapolis: Lerner Publications Co., Visual Geography Series, 1990.

Spini, Tito and Sandro. *Togu Na, The African Dogon "House of Men, House of Words."* New York: Rizzoli, 1976.

India

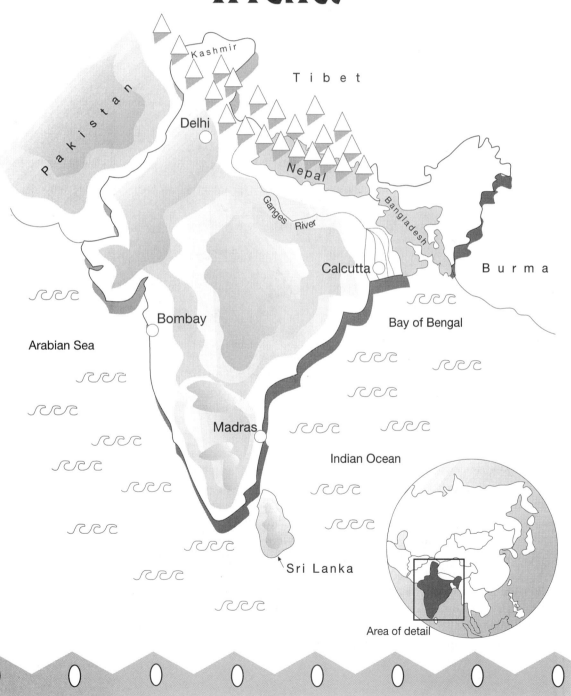

Kashmir

Tibet

Pakistan

Delhi

Nepal

Ganges River

Bangladesh

Burma

Calcutta

Bombay

Bay of Bengal

Arabian Sea

Madras

Indian Ocean

Sri Lanka

Area of detail

A BRIEF HISTORY OF INDIA

The peoples of India seem to be living in many centuries at once. Foreign visitors to the subcontinent (see Figure 6–1) are astounded to see that social, artistic, and ceremonial traditions that have evolved for five thousand years are still existing side by side with modern science and technology. The structure underlying this historical depth and richness of Indian life is Hinduism, the major religious tradition, which probably originated in the ancient Indus River valley civilization around 2500 B.C.

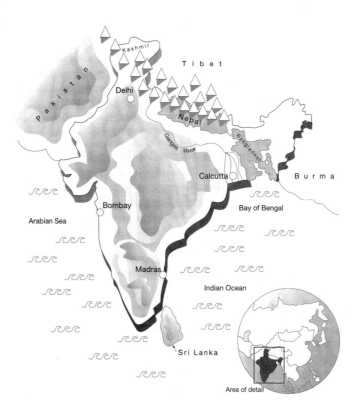

Figure 6-1. Map of India. This is a simplified locator map for quick reference. Students can look up a more detailed map of India in a world atlas.

When the Aryan peoples arrived from central Asia a thousand years later, their beliefs in many gods personifying the powers of nature augmented the old Hindu ritual practices. Aryans brought the Sanskrit language and the Vedas, or hymns, which have been transmitted by word of mouth for thousands of years, and still form a most sacred Hindu text. The Vedas codified the caste system whereby one's social class is determined at birth. The hierarchic ranking of the community into five categories—priests/Brahmins, warriors/Kshatriyas, merchants/Vaisyas, farmers/Sudras, and untouchables/Harijans—continues to this day.

Many gods and goddesses are worshipped in the polytheistic Hindu religion. Krishna is a favorite god, a god of joyous celebration who came to earth to teach divine bliss to humanity. (See Figure 6–2.) Always depicted as a blue being, Krishna multiplied himself so that he could make love to as many gopis, or cowgirls, as possible. The lessons he brings to mortals are the love of life and its analogy to the love of God.

Figure 6-2. In this contemporary painting from Nathdwara in Rajasthan, Krishna lifts the mountain on one finger. (Collection of Penny and David Dell.)

The Indian people's deep and abiding inclination to joy and celebration is manifested in abundant ritual celebrations with more than 360 different festivals celebrated every year. Festivals are ritual events that mark the cycle of the seasons—the solstices, the harvest, the movement of the sun. Each Hindu temple has an annual festival of its own particular diety.

Spectacular temple festivals, such as Rath Yatra at Puri, Orissa, on the east coast attract thousands of pilgrims from all parts of India. A rath is a ceremonial chariot forty feet high, with huge tall wheels, and at Puri, hundreds of devotees of the cult of Jagannath, an incarnation of Vishnu, pull three different chariots from one temple to another in the ritual celebrated every year in June–July. Gorgeous parades of worship and celebration are always part of the spectacle.

Fairs are more spontaneous celebrations by large congregations of people around a sacred site or market place. More than 400 different tribal groups participate in the exotic blend of cultures to be seen at these events. Fairs provide a space apart from the ordinary social constraints of this hierarchic society, where release is expressed in drama, dances, singing, and costume and body painting. Flower garlands and decorated animals, brilliant turbans and vibrantly colored saris, ornate decorations and caparisoned elephants celebrate the joyous pleasures of life encouraged by the Hindu philosophy.

ELEPHANTS IN INDIAN LIFE AND ART

Elephants are always included in the glittering festival processions, painted with floral motifs, and decked out with scarves, bells, lamps, garlands, pompoms, money, umbrellas, howdahs, tassels, necklaces, anklets, and whisks of yak tail or peacock feathers. (See Figures 6–3A and

Figure 6-3A. A regally attired elephant attends the palace in Jaiper. (Courtesy of Air India Library.)

Figure 6-3B. Painted elephant. (Courtesy of Air India Library.)

6–3B.) Elephants are the traditional transportation for the princes and maharajahs, and for wedding celebrations. Elephants also do the work of bulldozers and cranes on construction sites, contributing a powerful labor force to human plans.

Indian elephants have a mythic origin from the hands of Brahma. The grandeur of their enormous strength and size, their intelligence, and gentleness are virtues that have made them an embodiment of royal might and splendor. A white elephant is the symbolic vehicle of Indra. The Hindu god of wisdom and good fortune, Ganesha, has the head of an elephant. The elephant became a symbol of Buddha as well, and is represented in art to signify his presence.

The estimated 9,000 wild elephants remaining in India are protected in the hundreds of wildlife sanctuaries and national parks that have been established to conserve the abundant wildlife of India from encroachment by the increasing pressures of the population explosion. Poaching for the valuable ivory tusks is prohibited by conservation laws, but stakes are high and poachers have become more and more aggressive.

Hundreds of thousands of lovingly portrayed elephants are seen carved in stone in ancient temple reliefs over the entire Indian subcontinent. In the world's largest bas-relief, Arjuna's Penance, at Mahabalipuram on the Indian Ocean, the huge stone elephants gently guard and support a profusion of figures and animals. The sculptors of stone temples throughout the history of India have always been guided by ideals of quality workmanship prescribed in early sacred texts of art and architecture. Specific castes of stonecarvers have been active for centuries—the art has been passed down through the generations to those who are born into the stonecarver heritage.

Indian stonecarvers still stick to traditional forms, never following foreign-inspired forms. These sculptors have always lived and worked in proximity to temples, the source of their livelihood. Temple commissions are not so plentiful as they used to be, but they still carve replicas of the temples for the thriving tourist and pilgrim market, and carving for architectural ornamentation is still practiced.

Project 6–1: Carving an Elephant Bas-relief in Plaster

PREPARATION

Find pictures of elephants in the temple sculptures of India; they can be seen at Konarak, Ellora, Mahabalipuram, and Ajanta, for example. There are also thousands of elephant images in contemporary wall paintings, and in textiles, costume, and decorative arts. Photos of elephants in royal, religious, and wedding processions should not be difficult to locate.

MATERIALS

- plaster tablets (see note below)

  ## Make plaster blocks for carving as follows:

  1. Prepare simple molds from recycled cardboard boxes. Cereal boxes, for example, can be cut around the sides into two shallow containers for the plaster.
  2. Mix two parts of plaster to one part of warm water. Always add plaster to water, not the other way around. Pour plaster into water and mix with your hands until smooth and thick enough to coat your hand.
  3. Pour wet plaster into boxes to make plaques about 1/2 inch deep for carving reliefs.
  4. Let the plaster set up for 30 minutes or so before drawing on it. It will be soft like soap and easily carved for a day or two. Plaster will harden gradually, and can be carved at any stage.

- carving tools (can be almost any tool that is readily available, from spoon handles to kitchen knives to wooden skewers to clay modeling tools)
- shellac or acrylic medium

PROCEDURE

1. Make several sketches of elephants in order to bring a variety of visual information to your sculpture.
2. Sketch on the plaster.
3. Begin to engrave the design with tools.
4. Gradually develop the dimensional form of the figure in the plaster surface.
5. Keep refining the form and decoration until it is complete.
6. Protect the completed relief sculpture with two coats of shellac or acrylic medium.

CONCLUSION

Students can write an informative caption about the elephant image to display with their carved relief sculpture. Figure 6–4 shows an actual studio art project.

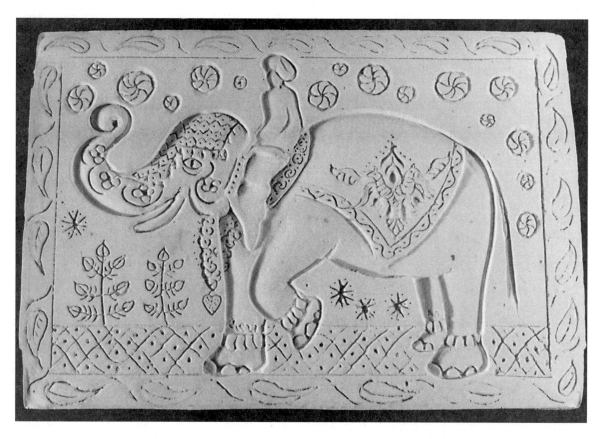

Figure 6-4. Studio art project. A festive elephant is carved in a plaster relief. (Artwork by Susan Hogan.)

FOLLOW-UP

Follow the trail of the elephant image to explore the varied art styles of different temples in India.

CREATIVE WRITING

Artisans who work with their hands are in the untouchable class. If you were a sculptor, what would you say to argue for equal status?

TEXTILE ARTS OF VILLAGE INDIA

One-seventh of the world's population, more than 615 million people, live in India's villages. Over many centuries the Indian peasants have evolved ways of living in harmony with natural resources and cycles of nature—enduring the extreme heat, drought and monsoon of the tropical and semi-tropical climate. The communities are conservative, retaining their same social customs generation after generation. Even city dwellers stay connected to their villages of origin as the source of their identity.

Rural Indians have traditionally adapted all available materials to practical uses within their villages. Every village has its own special craft skills, most often passed down by families as a continuing heritage. The incredible richness and variety of textile arts that are encountered in India has evolved from this focus by particular communities on the devoted practice of a particular style.

Gorgeous decoration of textiles is accomplished in a myriad of artful processes, including weaving, embroidery and appliqué, dyeing (tie and dye), ikat, batik, block printing, and painting. Handworked textiles become hangings, canopies, elephant gear, camel trappings, quilts, tablecloths, banners, tents, costumes, bedspreads, and clothing.

The sari in particular is the unique Indian dress—a length of beautiful cloth that women wrap around themselves as clothing. Saris are a fluid range of texture, embroidery, and pattern, but mostly vivid brilliant color. Sari shops in the United States offer a tremendous range of quality fabric lengths to be worn as dresses. Sari shops also import lavishly embroidered dresses that women in the Indian immigrant communities wear for special occasions.(See Figure 6–5A, 6–5B, and 6–5C.) Wedding celebrations are always an occasion for splendor in dress. The joy of lavishly ornamented attire makes the bride more desirable and gives her more status.

Project 6–2: Making a Mixed Media Collage Vest

Refer to the profusion of brilliant textile and costume arts for inspiration for this collage vest. Collage is liberating because students can use layers of all kinds of collected odds and ends to build up an ornate surface texture.

PREPARATION

Several picture books are available of the visual splendor of Indian festivals. Some tourist guides include vivid photos of Pongal and other celebrations; refer also to pictures of colorful flower garlands, paintings, decorations, feasts, garments, and processions to stimulate ideas.

MATERIALS

- an old shirt
- plastic bags
- scissors
- old odd pieces of jewelry
- sequins, buttons, shells, mica, beads
- adhesive: tacky glue, white glue, hot glue
- assorted fabrics
- felt, ribbons
- printed catalogs of jewelry
- fabric paint/gold

PROCEDURE

1. Cut the shirt into a vest shape by cutting a V-neck, cutting off the sleeves, and trimming the bottom into a pointed border.
2. Stuff the garment with plastic bags to make it easier to work on. Cut the fabrics into shapes that can be design elements in the first layer.
3. Start piling all the pieces you have collected on the vest.
4. Move things around, add a lot of things and take them away—keep working with your materials until a design begins to emerge.
5. Layer and blend a wide variety of colors and materials.
6. Start gluing the under layers; keep adding more elements on top.
7. Glue the remaining pieces and let it dry.
8. For a finishing touch, a squeeze bottle of fabric paint could be used to draw a design in gold over the entire vest collage.

CONCLUSION

Students can model their vests and discuss their potential as costumes. Figure 6–6 shows an actual studio art project.

FOLLOW-UP

"Paper dolls" can be used to illustrate students' further research into the ceremonial costume of India, including dances, puppets, and processions.

- Cut out fashion figures—either photos or illustrations.
- Use the cutout figures as stencils to trace around, to create a group composition (a tableau or dance).
- Use markers and collage to dress the figures in authentic costume.

CREATIVE WRITING

Describe your newly created vest. What special occasion(s) might you wear it to?

JEWELRY IN ANCIENT AND MODERN INDIA

We know that the Indian custom of wearing jewelry is 5,000 years old because of the abundant references to jewelry in ancient Indian literature, even in religious texts such as the Rig-Veda and Ramayana. The stone and metal sculptures of figures and animals in ancient temples frequently show very detailed depictions of jewelry. Many archaic forms and designs of jewelry portrayed in Indian miniature painting—the Mughal art of the fifteenth to nineteenth centuries—are still in use today. The conservatism of the rural women of India motivates them to take an active part in preserving traditional designs in all the arts. Their intention is, above all, to maintain the security of their way of life.

Ancient designs have profound symbolic meaning to the tribal people who continue to wear them. (See Figures 6–7A, 6–7B, and 6–7C.) Designs worn by all members of one group

Figures 6-5A, 6-5B, and 6-5C. Lavishly embroidered garments imported from India are displayed in a sari shop. (Courtesy of Krishna Sari Shop, Jersey City, New Jersey.)

Figure 6-6. Studio art project. All kinds of materials are combined in a rich surface texture adhered to a vest shape cut from an old shirt. (Artwork by Susan Hogan.)

Figure 6-7A. Gujerati women. (Courtesy of Air India Library.)

Figure 6-7B. Rajastani woman. (Courtesy of Air India Library.)

Figure 6-7C. Hindu bride. (Courtesy of Air India Library.)

create identity for each member of a particular group. Rural people place more trust in the steady tangible and visible value of jewelry than in the unpredictable value of currency. Jewelry also functions as an amulet: to protect the wearer from negative forces, such as witchcraft or illness, or to attract good fortune in the form of love, marriage, fertility, or business success. In Hindu practice, wearing an image of a deity is a form of worship and a solicitation of divine protection.

Parents of girls often array them with jewelry to make them more attractive to prospective marriage partners. Marriage is most important, and although the traditional customs are changing rapidly, most marriages are still arranged by the parents of the bride and groom. The dowry is the property and wealth the woman brings into the contract with the groom's family, and the type and value of precious metal jewelry is an important part of the deal. Until a very recent change in property law, the jewelry was the only wealth of her very own that a woman could possess without question. When the new bride goes to live in her husband's family household, it is important to wear all of her jewelry so that she will be accorded a higher status. It determines how the new family perceives her. The bride's jewelry is her protection against all misfortune, so that the new bride never removes it, even when bathing or sleeping.

Project 6–3: Making a Jewelry Collage

The Indian custom of personal ornamentation to celebrate the abundance and joy of life inspires this fantasy of lavish adornment with precious jewels, gold and silver. This project is an opportunity for students to imagine themselves as royalty, with the freedom to display all of their jewels at once. Encourage them to have fun attiring the paper model with a wealth of jewelled rings, chains, necklaces, bracelets, brooches, tiaras, etc.

PREPARATION

Have students assemble a collection of jewelry advertisements—which are readily available from catalogs, circulars and magazines—that have lavish photos of gems, crystals, and gold and silver chains. (Christmas is a good time of year to obtain this printed material.)

MATERIALS

- magazines and catalogs with abundant color photos of jewelry
- glue sticks
- scissors
- paper
- workable fixative
- watercolors or acrylics, brushes, water
- a fashion photo to use as the model (can be either a fashion photo or sketch from the newspaper, a self-portrait photo enlarged on the photocopier, or an image from the Indian miniature paintings, as long as the model's arms, neck, shoulders, head, and front torso are visible)

PROCEDURE

1. Paste your "model" photo to the page.
2. From a stack of photos of jewels and gems you have clipped from the printed sources, select jewels to arrange on the model. Collage allows the free play of trial and error in gradually developing the design and placement of elements that you like.
3. Use the glue stick to paste the jewelry onto the figure, and enjoy building up the jewelry texture to its maximum.
4. When the model cannot wear one more piece, spray the collage with workable fixative.
5. Add finishing touches. Use a thin wash of watercolor to tone the background with a color that sets off the subject. Tone the model's face and arms as well, if necessary.

CONCLUSION

Each student can cut out a paper frame for his or her collage. A display of the class work can be mounted. Figure 6–8 shows an actual studio art project.

FOLLOW-UP

- Have students create a personal picture file of interesting and beautiful images for collage materials for future projects.

Figure 6-8. Studio art project. Uses brilliant photographs of gold and jewels from jewelry advertisements to collage a vision of opulence. (Artwork by Susan Hogan.)

- Invite a jewelry business owner to come to talk to the class about jewelry importing and marketing.
- Assign research on the sources of gold, silver, gems, and cut stones for jewelry.
- Have students make a series of sketches of jewelry designs in Indian miniature paintings from the Rajput or Moghul styles.

CREATIVE WRITING

What do you think about the paradox that the poorest women in India deck themselves out in their best jewelry every day for every occasion? What identity are these women expressing?

Project 6–4: Making Découpage Arm Bangles

For the sheer fun of invention, encourage students to play with disposable, free materials in making arm bangles; using the leftover materials from the preceding jewelry collage project, paste them onto plastic bracelet rings. Then add three-dimensional elements such as stones, beads, shells, sequins, etc., to build up a textured surface.

See Figures 6–9A and 6–9B for actual arm bangles.

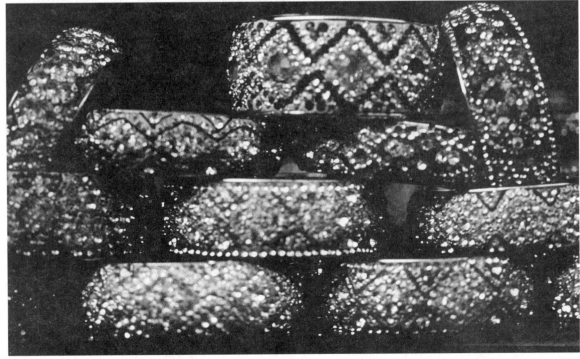

Figures 6-9A and 6-9B. Glittering arm bangles are for sale in Indian markets. (Courtesy of Air India Library.)

PREPARATION

The preceding project, especially the follow-up suggestions, works as preparation for this activity. Assemble collage materials before students begin.

MATERIALS

- slices of plastic bottles (1 liter or half liter, sliced in different widths)
- sharp blades and scissors
- gel medium or white glue
- brush
- leftover jewelry photos and a collection of small jewelry components (beads, old jewelry, sequins, stones, glass, etc.)
- gloss varnish

PROCEDURE

1. *Carefully* slice the bottles crosswise into rings with a sharp blade. (You can "cheat" by opening up the ring for an easier cut, then taping it together with transparent tape.)
2. Cover the rings with photo collage, using the acrylic gel medium or white glue.
3. Add three-dimensional bits to the collaged bracelets.
4. Build up layers of varied ornate texture.
5. Spray with gloss varnish.

CONCLUSION

Have the students exchange bangles, and take turns wearing as many of them as they can fit onto their arms at one time. Then try different ways of arranging them all together in an exhibit. Figure 6–10 shows an actual studio art project.

Figure 6-10. Studio art project. Rings sliced from plastic liter bottles are covered with photos, fabric, pebbles, glitter, and old jewelry to create a collection of ornate bangles. (Artwork by Susan Hogan, Marguerite Botto, Beverly Fuchsman, and Mary Ann Rich.)

FOLLOW-UP

The exuberance of playing with throwaway stuff confers freedom. This creative exercise can be an effective warm-up for serious jewelry design in more traditional materials. Or it can be a starter for more creative costume jewelry inventions, including pendants and headpieces.

CREATIVE WRITING

Playing with the fantasy of tangible wealth such as gems, jewels, gold, and silver, write about the experience of being great royalty with piles of riches in India's mythic past.

PAINTED HOMES OF VILLAGE INDIA

The daily art of women is a common thread that ties together the very diverse cultures of India. The women of almost every household in village India—one-sixth of all the women in the world—decorate the walls and floors of their homes with auspicious motifs. Their regular painting expresses their devotion to home and family in a ritual to cleanse and beautify the domestic space and to invoke blessing for all who live within it.

These painted decorations have different names in different regions. Each region across the vast area from the desert of the Northwest to the jungle villages of the Southeast has a unique style, and each household has its own variations of it. Knowledge of the art has been passed from mother to daughter across countless past generations. Women are the authorities of family tradition. They are responsible for maintaining customs and beliefs; thus, they insure the well-being of family and community.

Most of their ornamental painting is devoted to Lakshmi, the goddess of abundance and prosperity, with the belief that she will respond with blessing and protection for the home. Elephants and peacocks, in particular, are images that beckon her attention.

White—considered pure and sacred—is the most common color. Rice powder or paste is applied where it is available; otherwise, white chalk or lime is used. Colored powders can be purchased in the market for special occasions. The colors are applied directly to the surface of walls and floors with a homemade brush, a rag, or fingers.

In the state of Tamil Nadu, India's southernmost state, painted floor decorations are called rangolis. (See Figure 6–11.) They are made by mothers and daughters every morning before sunrise to bring good into the home. Motifs painted on the ground in front of the entrance include geometric designs (6-pointed stars), and endless variaties of leaves, flowers, vines, figures, animals, and birds. Foot traffic during the day obliterates these paintings, which are then renewed each morning. At Pongal (the harvest festival), larger and more elaborate paintings (as wide as the streets where the temple chariots pass) are made of colored powder on the earth to honor the sun's movement along the zodiac.

Project 6–5: Painting on Sidewalks and Parking Lots

The perennial cycles of the sun, moon, and planets throughout the days, the seasons, and the years are acknowledged and honored in this folk art of Indian women. Have students consider the circular nature of the earth and of the planetary movements as you prepare to make drawings on the ground. As more and more of our world is paved over, making temporary works of art on these public surfaces can be a way of confronting, and questioning the alarming effects of too many cars in our world.

PREPARATION

Before doing this project, you need to obtain permission from the principal to use the sidewalks and/or parking lot. Look at pictures of Indian village art for inspiration. Have students draw simple circular motifs to represent the earth's revolutions in relation to the sun, moon, and stars through time.

MATERIALS

- sidewalk chalk or colored chalk (or simply use sticks of white chalk)
- open paved area

PROCEDURE

1. Your teacher will find an available expanse of paved surface on which your class will draw.
2. Each student will be assigned a separate area.
3. Warm up by drawing freely and expressively with the chalk.
4. When time is up, walk around and look at each other's work.
5. In a second session, your class will develop the project in a more structured way.
   Use the theme of cycles/circular movement in making geometric chalk drawings.

CONCLUSION

The students can walk from one chalk drawing to the next as they compare the results of the two different approaches.

Record the pavement painting process in photographs or on videotape. Record the works as they progress and the student discussion of the outcome.

Figures 6–12A and 6–12B show actual studio art projects.

FOLLOW-UP

- Artists in France and Italy use colored chalk to make elaborate copies of old master paintings on sidewalks in tourist areas. More developed chalk paintings could be assigned if students are interested in the possibilities of this approach.
- Consider having your students paint circular motifs/themes on cafeteria or hallway walls. These murals could be part of a multicultural celebration with other cultures represented.

CREATIVE WRITING

Write about graffiti on public property. What motivates graffiti? Why is it considered an offensive art form? What is the difference between this chalk painting on pavement and spray-paint graffiti?

Figure 6-11. Rangolis from a village in South India are renewed daily as an expression of devotion. (Photographs by Kathy Butterly.)

Figures 6-12A and 6-12B. Studio art project. Circular designs drawn with colored chalk on pavement address the themes of rotation, orbit, and cycles in time. (Artwork by Susan Hogan and Anique Taylor.)

Vocabulary Worksheet for India

Look up the following vocabulary words in a dictionary, write the definition, and then use the word in writing a sentence about India. Use a separate sheet of paper for this activity.

amulet	livelihood
bas-relief	maharajas
Brahma	monsoon
Buddha	Mughal art
caparisoned	myriad
castes	poaching
cults	polytheistic
deity	rangoli
dowry	replicas
exotic	ritual
Ganesha	saris
Hindu	solicitation
howdahs	solstices
Indra	subcontinent
Krishna	untouchable

Geography Worksheet for India

Find the answers to these problems in world atlases and encyclopedias. Use the back of this sheet if you need more space.

- What area is politically allied with India but geographically part of Tibet?

  _____

  _____

- What attracted the British to colonize India, and which cities did they establish? Which cities were established by other European colonizers?

  _____

  _____

- Locate the many wildlife preserves that have been established throughout the country, and find out about the wildlife that is protected there.

  _____

  _____

- Choose one state to research: report on its location, borders, geographic features, climate, population centers, natural resources, and culture.

- What are monsoons, when do they appear, and how do they affect the seasons in India?

  _____

  _____

- What two countries were partitioned from India in the twentieth century?

  _____

  _____

- Nomadic peoples still inhabit what region of India?

  _____

  _____

Geography Worksheet for India (continued)

- Take a float trip all the way down the Ganges from its source to the ocean. Write a travel article describing the places you pass through.

  _____

  _____

- Plan a journey through Kashmir. Describe what you would see and where you would go and the different terrain and geographic areas you would travel through. What are the political and cultural conflicts there?

  _____

  _____

Name _____ Date _____

Related Assignments for India

1. **History**. Make a timeline painting of Indian history.

2. **Travelogue**. Plan a trip through India for a particular purpose: art research, village India, comparative religion, pilgrimage, architectural study, language.

3. **Ecology**. What is being done to preserve endangered species of wildlife in India, such as the Bengal tiger and the one-horned rhino?

4. **Architecture**
   - Taj Mahal
   - "Bombay Gothic"
   - the palaces of Udaipur and Jaipur that have been renovated as hotels

5. **Literature**
   - Upanishads
   - Rudyard Kipling, *Jungle Book*
   - E. M.Forster, *A Passage to India*

6. **Biography**
   - Mahatma Gandhi
   - Mother Teresa
   - Rabindranath Tagore
   - Jawaharlal Nehru
   - Emperor Shah Jahan
   - Indira Gandhi

7. **Economics**. Plan a presentation for craft products of India at an international trade fair. Where would you get information for setting up an export business?

RESOURCES FOR TEACHING

BOOKS

Barnard, Nicholas. *Arts & Crafts of India*. London: Conran Octopus, 1993.

Eames, Andrew (ed.). *India, Insight Guides*. Boston: Houghton Mifflin, 1996.

Holidays, Festivals, and Celebrations of the World Dictionary. Compiled by Sue Ellen Thompson and Barbara W. Carlson. Detroit: Omnigraphics, Inc., 1994.

Huyler, Stephen. *Painted Prayers: Women's Art in Village India*. New York: Rizzoli, 1994.

Oliphant, Margaret. *The Atlas of the Ancient World*. New York: Simon & Schuster, 1992. (Also appropriate for China, Maya, and Turkey.)

Robinson, Andrew. *Maharaja, The Spectacular Heritage of Princely India*. New York: Vendome Press, 1988.

VIDEOTAPES

Chasing India's Monsoon, World of Discovery, ABC/Kane Productions, 1992.

North India, Varanasi to the Himalayas, Lonely Planet, International Video Network, 1995.

The Jewel in the Crown, Masterpiece Theatre Series, 1984

TOURIST OFFICE

India Government Tourist Office
30 Rockefeller Plaza
New York, NY 10112
(212) 586-4901

BOOKSTORE

The Asia Society Bookstore
725 Park Avenue
New York, NY 10021
(212) 288-6400

MUSEUM RESOURCES

Arthur M. Sackler Gallery
Smithsonian Institution
Washington, D.C. 20560

CURRICULUM MATERIALS

Asian Studies Curriculum Center
New York University
635 East Building
New York, NY 10003
(212) 998-5497

BIBLIOGRAPHY

Barnard, Nicholas. *Arts & Crafts of India*. London: Conran Octopus, 1993.

Bussabarger, Robert F. *The Everyday Art of India*. New York: Dover, 1968.

Edwardes, Michael. *Indian Temples and Palaces*. London: Paul Hamlym, 1969.

Finlay, Hugh, et al. *India a Travel Survival Kit*. Hawthorne, Australia: Lonely Planet, 1993.

Huyler, Stephen. *Painted Prayers: Women's Art in Village India*. New York: Rizzoli, 1994.

Huyler, Stephen. *Village Life in India*. New York: Abrams, 1981.

Iyer, K. Bharatha. *Animals in Indian Sculpture*. Bombay: Taraporevala, 1977.

Kennett, Frances. *Ethnic Dress*. New York: Facts on File, 1995.

Mack, John (ed.). *Ethnic Jewelry*. New York: Abrams, 1988.

Robinson, Andrew. *Maharaja, The Spectacular Heritage of Princely India*. New York: Vendome Press, 1988.

Ypma, Herbert J. M. *India Modern: Traditional Forms and Contemporary Design*. London: Phaidon Press, Ltd., 1994.

Zimmer, Heinrich. *The Art of Indian Asia*. (vol 2.) New York: Bollingen, 1955.

Tibet

Area of detail

People's
Republic
of China

People's
Republic
of China

Indus River

Yangtze River

△ Mt. Kailash
(*Kangrinpoche*)

○ Amdo

Salween River

Mekong River

India

Brahmaputra River

○ Lhasa

Nepal

△
Mt. Everest
(*Qomolangma*)

Bhutan

Myanmar

India

A BRIEF HISTORY OF TIBET

Tibet is known as the "Rooftop of the World" because it occupies the highest land mass on Earth. The highest Himalayan mountain peaks, including Mt. Everest, are located within its borders. Many other extremely high mountain ranges include the Karakorum, Kunlan, and Min Shan. The melted snows of Tibetan mountain ranges become some of the great rivers of Asia: the Indus, the Ganges, the Yangtze, the Mekong, and the Brahmaputra. North of central Tibet is the vast and barren Changthang, the highest and largest plateau in the world. (See Figure 7–1.)

Figure 7-1. Map of Tibet. Tibet is officially and politically considered part of China. This is a locator map for quick reference. Students can look up a more detailed map of Tibet (see China maps) in a world atlas.

On the high plains, vegetation is sparse, and nomads still herd their flocks of sheep, goats, and yaks from one grazing area to another, much as they have for a thousand years. The yak is particularly well adapted to thrive in Tibet's high altitudes, and provides a full range of necessities for nomadic life. Butter made from yak milk is the nomads' staple food, made into the butter tea which is consumed in great quantity throughout the day. The coarse black yak hair is the raw material from which tents are made. Yak hides are used to construct lightweight, portable boats called *coracles*, needed to cross the many rivers. In spite of the political turmoil across Tibet in recent decades, the nomads have been able to retain much of their traditional lifestyle. Their ideal is still to achieve a full life in harmonious balance with nature.

In past centuries Tibet's high and remote location generally protected it from influence by the outside world. Its natural geographic isolation supported the unique development of state bureaucracy unified with a religious heirarchy. The country was officially closed to foreigners. Early in the twentieth century, intrepid British traders extended their influence from India to establish a network of trade channels. In the 1940s, Heinrich Harrer, a German refugee from British India, fled across the Himalayas and overcame unbelievable difficulties to make his way to Lhasa, capital city of Tibet and center of its Tibetan Buddhist hierarchy.

Gradually Harrer won the confidence of the fourteenth Dalai Lama, and became his English tutor. In his book *Seven Years in Tibet*, Harrer narrates his fascinating story of life in Lhasa in the years before the Chinese Communist invasion.

Tibet has a long and tumultuous history with China. China considered Tibet part of its own territory, but Tibetans consider their country a sovereign and distinct entity, and have not accepted Chinese dominance.

The *Dalai Lama*, traditional high priest and king and ultimate ruler of all of Tibet, at first attempted to compromise and to coexist with Chinese rule, but eventually had to flee the Chinese in 1959. The government of India offered asylum, and the Dalai Lama set up a Tibetan government in exile in Dharamsala, northern India. He has continued negotiations with the Chinese, but an acceptable agreement that would provide for his protected return to Lhasa has never been reached.

From his Tibetan Buddhist center in Dharamsala, His Holiness the fourteenth Dalai Lama has continued to actively strive for world peace. In response to Chinese oppression, he teaches the Buddhist way of cultivating inner peace by overcoming anger, pride, and ignorance. In 1989, his dedication was recognized by the Nobel Peace Prize.

Since the Chinese occupation of Tibet in 1959, more of the land is exploited. The Chinese habit of intensive land-use is in complete opposition to traditional Tibetan low-intensity habitation. The Chinese have altered agricultural practices to increase yields, and have conducted extensive prospecting for natural resources: gold, uranium, coal, hydropower, precious metals, and wildlife, which China needs to support development for its huge population and to achieve power in world politics and trade.

The Chinese "cultural revolution" from 1966 until 1976 under Mao Zedong destroyed most monasteries and forbade traditional religious practices. A change of policy in the 1980s allowed the restoration of monasteries, and Tibetans have been rebuilding their traditional religious centers. A visitor to Tibet today may again see the prayer flags, prayer wheels, altars, shrines, and ceremonies, a resurgence of lives suffused with Buddhist devotion. (See Figure 7–2.)

TIBETAN BUDDHISM

In the seventh century, Songtsen Gampo, Tibet's powerful king and the most influential ruler in Central Asia, decided to promote peace by introducing Buddhism into Tibet. He married two foreign wives—the Chinese Princess Wen Chang and the Nepalese Princess Bhrikuti, both of whom followed the Buddha's teachings. They each arrived in Lhasa with retinues of Buddhist scholars and artists, as well as the first Buddhist images, bringing their respective cultures into Tibetan aristocratic and religious life. The Tibetan people perceived both of them as incarnations of Tara Dolma, their Savioress from Earthly Misery. From Songtsen Gampo's wives, Buddhism became a distinctive and powerful religious force in the formation of Tibetan identity.

Thousands of dieties can be identified in the Tibetan pantheon of gods, made visible in their art forms, which have traditionally been such an integral part of daily life. Buddhist doctrine and iconography, imported from India via Nepal, incorporated the vital energy of the local gods and beliefs of the native Bon religion. This combination of religious fervor with distinctive geography nurtured the development of the uniquely Tibetan Buddhism, so profusely expressed for many centuries in its sacred art and monastic architecture.

Figure 7-2. The Wheel of Existence, 18th-early 19th century. Yama, the Lord of Death, holds the Tibetan Buddhist wheel of endless incarnations, showing realms of the gods, titans, pretas, hell dwellers, animals, and humans set in landscape and architecture of the local Tibetan scene. (Photograph by Sunami. Collection of the Newark Museum, Newark, New Jersey. Purchase, 1936.)

TIBETAN TANKAS

bKra-sis-bDe-legs (pronounced Tashi delek)

translated into English:

"May you have good fortune, happiness, and all blessings"

An inscription on a Tibetan tanka, a painting intended to bear such blessing into the world.

Tibetan tankas are paintings on cloth that present the Buddhist teachings in visible form. They are symbolic picture-tools painted to inform the thoughts of Tibetan devotees. The representations of Buddhas and saints in ideal worlds are intended to become an actual sacred space for the enlightened ones to inhabit. The meditator on these ideal beings is enabled to actually imagine their presence and recreate the transcendent world in his or her own mind.

Paradise of Green Tara from the Newark Museum collection (see Figure 7–3) seems to be a female manifestation of the red form of the Buddha (Amitabha), who is seated under the golden dome at the very top of the heavenly palace. Her lotus throne presents her as an enlightened being. The glow of her body halo is the emanation of great light from her presence. Adorned, Nepalese style, with golden necklaces and pendants, beautiful flowers at her shoulders, and a streaming red scarf garment, she wears a crown of golden ornaments on her flowing dark blue hair. In the center of her forehead is the vertical third eye of infinite vision.

The presence of the Green Tara is surrounded by attendants who celebrate and support her divine appearance. Groups of four angels playing musical instruments appear both right and left in the garden. Heavenly beings in the clouds above bear fans, banners, and instruments, while arhats, the Tibetan saints, confer. In circles at each top corner are four Buddhas seated on lotus thrones.

The Green Tara's paradise is intensely green, the ease of a lush and verdant world imagined in a barren land, set off by the contrasting bright red fences and structures, and dark blue accents. The mythical green trees wear garlands of wish-granting jewels. The pool where the lotuses grow is a sacred emblem in the high and dry desert where water is precious. White clouds are delicately modulated tints of blue and silver.

Two Wrathful Dieties depicted in the bottom corners protect the entrance to this paradise. The angry dark blue god on the lower left, mounted on a horse and wielding a *dorje*, wears a crown of skulls, a flayed tiger pelt around her waist, and a writhing halo of blue flames or smoke. The white god on the lower right, mounted on a lion, also wears a tiger pelt. He has six arms, three faces, and three eyes per angry face. Just behind these terrorizing figures we see a peaceful couple of elephants on the right and a lovely pair of peacocks on the left. (See Figure 7–4.)

When this tanka was painted, in the eighteenth century, it was then consecrated in a ritual inviting the goddess to enter the painting. Where it is viewed in a ceremony of devotion, the blessing of the green Tara is extended to those who contemplate her image. In meditation practice, this tanka serves as an aid to visualizing the paradise of the goddess in complete detail, so that it becomes vividly real in the heart of the devotee.

Tankas are painted on coarse linen that has been primed with chalk mixed with glue. Designs are transferred to the surface from patterns: the eternally perfect proportions of the Buddha are thus transmitted century after century without change. They are painted with bright water-soluble paints. When finished, the painting is sewn into an ornate silk mounting.

Figure 7-4. Paradise of Green Tara, tanka detail.

Project 7–1: Painting an Ideal World

PREPARATION

Study the images of Paradise in this tanka, and discuss the concept of an ideal world. As students consider the possibility of visualizing heaven on Earth, they should start to imagine what they might include, and how they would build this vision.

MATERIALS

- paper and pencils for sketching the individual designs
- a tracing wheel to puncture the design outlines
- powdered charcoal or chalk to pounce the design
- tempera paints, or fabric paints
- brushes
- mixing bowls for paint and containers for water
- a white sheet from the thrift shop, or a large white muslin cloth
- stapler to stretch the cloth

Figure 7-3. Paradise of Green Tara, Tibetan tanka. (Collection of the Newark Museum, Newark, New Jersey. Shelton Collection, 1920.)

- gesso to prime the support
- black marking pens
- dish detergent
- masking tape
- iron
- blanket binding and bamboo pole or curtain rod

PROCEDURE

1. Develop images of visible ideals in a series of sketches, and then decide on a relative size or scale for each image.
2. On the completed drawing, puncture the outlines with a tracing wheel. This is the technical procedure used in authentic tanka painting, and in Western culture in scene painting.
3. Spread the sheet or cloth out on the floor, and tape it down firmly.
4. Prime the cloth by painting it with gesso. Allow to dry.
5. You and your classmates should place all the drawings on the sheet and move around in the process of developing a balanced and harmonious composition for the Paradise banner.
6. Some of the motifs can be repeated two or several times to create a full and rhythmic composition.
7. When the placement of the images has been resolved, "pounce" them with powdered charcoal to transfer the design to the cloth. Pouncing is done with powdered charcoal in a small cloth pouch which is dabbed along the perforated pattern line, leaving a dotted line on the cloth beneath.
8. This preliminary charcoal transfer can be erased, changed, and adjusted.
9. When resolved, outline the images with a black marking pen.
10. Decide on a color scheme. Use the Tibetan tankas for inspiration, and review the specific color symbolism.
11. Before using the paint on the large cloth, make a trial piece by trying the paint at different levels of saturation to find out how best to apply it. Find the optimum level of dilution for the paint and the cloth. Add a bit of dish detergent to break the surface resistance when the paint is brushed onto the cloth.
12. Use diluted tempera paints to paint the composition. Fabric paints are a more durable and flexible alternative.
13. Iron the finished painting to set the colors and to render the fabric flexible.
14. Attach a casing of blanket binding to the back of the banner, and then insert a bamboo pole or a curtain rod for hanging.

CONCLUSION

When the complete painting is on display, discuss with the students the Buddhist concept of consecrating it. Is there a comparable procedure that is followed in our own culture?

Students can research pictures of Paradise in other cultures, such as Persia or Japan, and write a description of its features.

CREATIVE WRITING

Write a press release publicizing the exhibit of the banner. How would you present this paradise painting to the world?

TIBETAN CEREMONIAL INSTRUMENTS

Skulls, blood, and flayed human skins are emblems of the Wrathful Dieties, protectors of the faith who guard against harm. In these symbols of confrontation with death of the human body are remnants of powerful forces of the ancient Bon religion, which have been incorporated into Buddhism. These images of terror and physical mutilation preserve the mystery and magic of death, blood, and bones, translating the old rituals of sacrifice into symbolic forms appropriate for the later, nonviolent religion.

For many centuries, the custom of *sky burial* has been practiced in Tibet. After their funeral services, dead bodies are placed on a consecrated site to be eaten by vultures. The sky is the pervasive symbol of liberation of one's consciousness from attachment to the body into the celestial realm. Tibetans believe that offering corpses to the birds brings merit and benefit both to the dead person and to those who carry out the ceremony. Witnessing sky burial brings home the transience of human life, and convinces any viewer not to waste one moment of life on this earth. Sky burial is also a very efficient means of disposing of corpses. Not only would it be too difficult to dig holes in the rocky ground, but Mother Earth is sacred to Tibetan Buddhists, and not to be defiled with dead bodies. Cremation would be very expensive because fuel is so scarce. Sky burial insures that the corpse is totally removed from the physical world.

In these ceremonial death rites, bones of very special individuals can be saved and used in implements of significant power. The monks' ritual dances in skeleton regalia using these implements of bone seem to be a confrontation with death, challenging the universal human fear of it. These rites are secrets; they are not divulged by monks and not widely known among Tibetans.

Dakinis, or spirits, appear in paintings and sculpture holding *skull drums* in their hands. (See Figure 7–5.) Tibetan skull drums, thigh bone trumpets, and bone aprons and belts are displayed in museums and seen in auction catalogs, but their significance in ritual use is not generally known.

Project 7–2: Making a Tibetan Skull Drum

PREPARATION

Study reproductions of Tibetan paintings to identify different implements used by the dakinis, or guardian spirits. Can students identify figures holding skull drums? Can they guess what the significance of this emblem might be in its pictorial context?

Figure 7-5. Skull drums are ceremonial musical instruments of Tibet. (Photograph by Bob Hanson. Collection of the Newark Museum, Newark, New Jersey. Skull drum: Crane Collection, 1911. Rattle drum: Mathilde Oestrich Bequest Fund, 1972.)

MATERIALS

- small bowls: plastic, styrofoam, or paper
- Celluclay™ or Sculptamold™
- sandpaper (medium to fine grit)
- acrylic gel medium
- thin leather or latex for the drumheads
- ribbon or thin strip of leather for the center band
- shells for decoration
- small stones and string for beaters
- an old silk necktie to recycle
- scissors
- elastic bands to hold the leather in place as it dries, if necessary

PROCEDURE

1. Trim the edges of two small plastic bowls. They should be at least 2 inches deep.
2. Glue the bowls together at the base using gel medium, and let dry.
3. Coat the double bowl form with Celluclay™ pulp or Sculptamold™, smoothing the surface as it dries. It may take a few hours to dry hard.
4. Sand the surface, and coat with shellac or with acrylic medium.
5. Place the drum on thin leather, and trace around the circle.
6. Add 1/4 inch extra around the edge, and cut out two circles for the drum heads.
7. Adhere the leather to the plastic bowls by applying a thin strip of gel medium on the outside edge of each bowl.
8. Place the leather over the bowl and press the edges of the leather circle into the gel to glue it on.
9. Stretch it firmly, and hold in place with an elastic band.
10. When dry, the excess leather can be trimmed off.
11. Make the beaters by wrapping two small stones with string and painting the wrapped stone with acrylic gel medium. Let dry. There should be at least 3 inches of string attached to each one.
12. Place the strip of cloth around the center where the two bowls join.
13. Attach the beaters to the cloth strip, on opposite sides, with staples, glue, or needle and thread.
14. Decorate the center strip by gluing shells to it.
15. Add a decorative silk sash to the drum by using a cut-up old silk necktie.

CONCLUSION

Now that students have made their own skull drums, have them research some of the popular ceremonies performed by the Tibetan monks. What function do they serve for Buddhist devotees? Figure 7–6 shows a skull drum made as a studio art project.

Figure 7-6. Studio art project. This skull drum is made of plastic bowls, leather, silk necktie, ribbon, yarn, shells, and stones.

FOLLOW-UP

How could students invent other fanciful instruments using plastic bowls and cups, by cutting them up and combining them, and adding functional elements like strings, rattles, and festive decorations?

CREATIVE WRITING

Write down your thoughts about using human bones and skulls to make instruments.

TIBETAN CARPETS

In the vast Asian territory from Turkey to Mongolia, called the *steppes* of Central Asia, rugs were developed for warmth and comfort over centuries of time. All nomadic peoples of Central Asia are herders—they spin the wool of their flocks of sheep, goats, and yaks into yarn, and weave rugs on looms that are a part of their traveling equipment. Carpets are ideal portable furniture for tents. Weaving rugs for beds and seating, pillows and blankets, saddle blankets, and stove covers maintains the self-sufficiency of the nomadic economy. In the stark semi-arid landscape of this part of the world, the thick plush patterns and colors of the hand-woven carpets, packed along on yak-back, provide instant home decoration in the yak-hair tents that are moved from place to place with the grazing herds.

Many aspects of the long history and tradition of the Tibetans are expressed in both the distinctive rug-weaving techniques and the symbolic designs woven into their carpets. Some carpets are ceremonial in use. The lotus, the peony, the dragon, clouds and rainbows—motifs that are also seen in the carpets of China—are sacred Buddhist symbols that are not supposed to be walked or sat upon. The Tiger Rugs are interpretations of tiger pelts, ceremonial items that confer authority on those who possess them, symbolizing access to the power and strength of the tiger. This tiger also signifies the ego and the need to overcome the wild forces in the psyche to achieve enlightenment.

Carpets have also become a valuable product to trade for other necessities. This traditional Tibetan nomadic art has been carried into their life in exile into India and Nepal, where Tibetan refugees from the Chinese takeover of Tibet now produce carpets for sale worldwide.

Tibetan rugs now woven are thicker and plusher than other Asian carpets due to the unique technique of double knotting that they use. Figures 7–7A through 7–7D show several adaptations of classical rug designs woven in Tibet now, and exported to worldwide markets by Gangchen Carpets of Tibet. They represent a contemporary integration of classical Tibetan motifs into fashion for home decoration.

Figure 7-7A. "Tibetan sky." Tibetan carpet evokes the beauty of Tibet's brilliant blue sky, often filled with fantastic and unique cloud formations. The cloud motif is a popular design element in Tibetan carpets, textiles, paintings, and architecture. (Courtesy of Gangchen Carpets of Tibet, Inner Asia Trading Company.)

Figure 7-7B. "Classic Tibetan Floral." Classic design of 1930s' weaving combines motifs of lotus, cloud, water, and rock. (Courtesy of Gangchen Carpets of Tibet, Inner Asia Trading Company.)

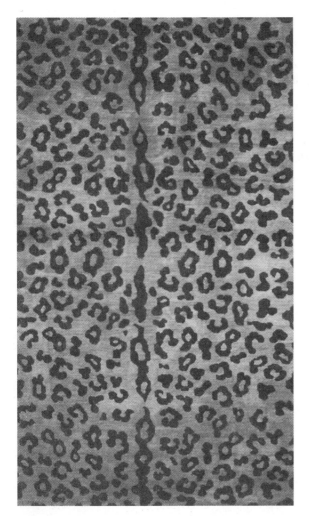

Figure 7-7C. "Snow Leopard." Snow leopards are the most elusive of Tibet's wildlife, and blend perfectly into their environment. This design is an expression of support for the preservation of the snow leopard, now an endangered species. (Courtesy of Gangchen Carpets of Tibet, Inner Asia Trading Company.)

Figure 7-7D. "Tiger." Inspired by the antique tiger rugs of Tibet, which were believed to have the power to fend off evil spirits. For Buddhists, the tiger rug is a constant reminder that our passionate ego is an obstacle in the path to enlightenment. (Courtesy of Gangchen Carpets of Tibet, Inner Asia Trading Company.)

Project 7–3: Painting a Tibetan Tiger Rug

PREPARATION

Collect pictures for design resources: pictures and photos of tigers, leopards, and snow leopards can be found in encyclopedias, picture books of wildlife, or children's books about animals.

Discuss the category of tiger rugs and their symbolic function in Tibetan tradition.

Warm up for painting on carpet with dry media by having students try out the materials first. On scraps of carpet, try the pastels or colored chalks and markers to get a feel for the process and to get a sense of how the project will look.

NOTE

Demonstration by the teacher helps free the student to plunge into working from a source if the teacher demonstrates a freely interpretative approach, by looking at the source and beginning to sketch the broad outlines, verbalizing the process, and declaring an ease and a confidence that will develop once the initial steps have been made.

MATERIALS

- paper and charcoal to sketch from picture resources
- carpet remnants or samples in neutral colors, about 2' by 3'
- colored chalk or pastels, some markers
- scissors
- water spray bottle
- hair dryer
- spray fixative
- white glue
- casing—blanket binding or strip of heavy fabric
- rod for hanging finished work

PROCEDURE

1. Glue a casing to the back at the top of the rug in order to insert a rod for hanging all the rugs in a display.
2. Referring to the tiger resources you have gathered in preparation, sketch the image, modify it, simplify it, and resolve it into a strong model.
3. Selecting the best visual idea, make the drawing more complete and to scale.
4. Cut out the drawing for a pattern.
5. Place it onto the carpet and trace around it with chalk.
6. Select a color scheme.
7. Color in the image, details, and background with colored chalk and/or markers.
8. Fix by spritzing with water.
9. Dry with a hair dryer.
10. Build up more color if desired.
11. Finish with a clear matte fixative spray, or Scotchgard®.

Notes on Working on Carpet

Short pile or uncut pile is easier to work on and doesn't eat up the chalk sticks so fast; the results are sharper detail. Longer shag gives a fuzzy effect. Spray with water sets the pastel. Wait until it is DRY to build up another layer. Spray with water when complete. Let it DRY completely, then spray with acrylic fixative or hair spray. Experiment with sealer sprays. Figure 7–8 shows an actual studio art project of a tiger rug.

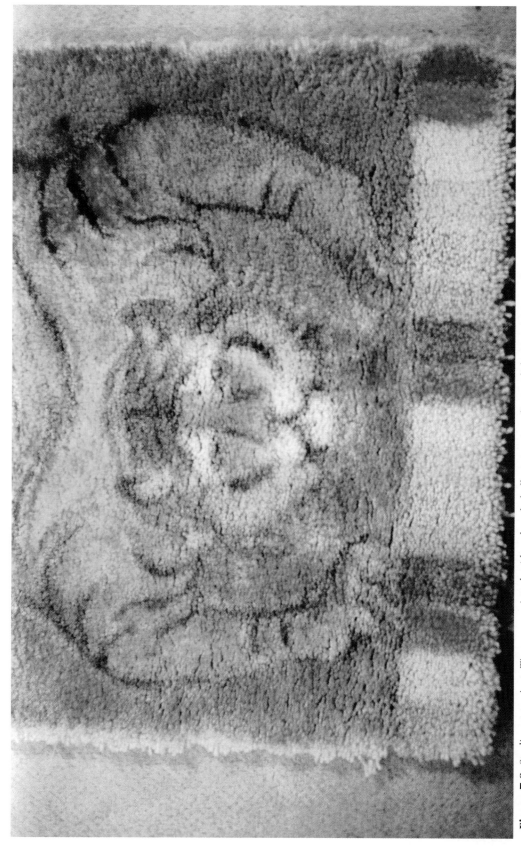

Figure 7-8. Studio art project. Tiger rug painted with colored chalk on carpet. (Artwork by Susan Hogan.)

Other Options

- Students can work in pairs to work more quickly or in order to create larger rugs.
- A tiger skin design can be cut out as a silhouette.

How Long Does this Project Take?

Set up a timetable: picture research, sketches, making a final design, adding a horizontal tube for hanging on the back, cutting it out as a pattern to trace onto the carpet, pastel painting the complete rug, spraying to set, building up more color, spraying and drying again, spray sealer final coat.

CONCLUSION

Discuss the actual tiger in Tibetan wildlife and what has happened to them since the Chinese takeover.

FOLLOW-UP

Visit the local carpet store, department store, or home furnishings store to look at a wide range of rug designs; notice the great variations of texture, color, and design in rugs from different countries. A field trip can open up a new resource for design, and promote appreciation of the cultural variations in world traditions of carpets.

CREATIVE WRITING

Write an imaginary TV news magazine segment about rugs from Tibet including references to customs, symbols, wildlife, international trade, etc.

METALWORKING TRADITIONS IN TIBET

The traditional craft of metalworking in Tibet has a history of over a thousand years, and continues at a very high level of quality to this day. Tibetan monasteries are packed full of sculptures in gold and silver: there are thousands of images of the deities, ornate altars, and the *stupas*, or tombs, of all the preceding Dalai Lamas. The monastery rooftops are lavishly ornamented with metal sculptures, borders, and gargoyles. On the practical side, household necessities such as teapots, incense burners, and cooking ware are still abundantly handcrafted, and uniquely Tibetan in design.

Gold and silver ornaments of all kinds are to be found in the markets. Jewelry and body ornamentation became more and more elaborate to express the wearer's identity. Jewelry safely carried on the body is also a way of storing personal wealth, as in India.

Handcrafted prayer wheels were always an important product in Buddhist Tibet. The copper or brass rotating drums were carried and used by almost everyone in their daily devotions. We don't know whether Tibetans have been allowed to continue this religious practice by the occupying Chinese. Charmboxes (see Figure 7–9) are still popular items, traditionally worn around the neck as a pendant or attached to the belt to keep the amulets of protection close to the wearer's body. Their widespread use is evidence of the combination of shamanism and superstition—to ward off bad luck—with the later practice of Buddhism.

Figure 7-9. Tibetan Silver Charmbox, early 20th century, silver and gold on copper. (Photograph by Armen. Collection of the Newark Museum, Newark, New Jersey. Purchase, 1979. W. Clark Symington Bequest Fund.)

Project 7–4: Making a Copper Repoussé Plaque

Repoussé is the French word for embossed, and it means literally "pushed out." Metal embossing is done on thin sheet metal with simple wooden modeling tools.

Eight Glorious Buddhist Emblems. These eight symbols—lotus, wheel, banner or standard, vase, umbrella, fish, conch, and endless knot—have profound significance in Tibetan life. (See Figures 7–10A and 7–10B.) You can see them painted on walls, appliqued on tents and awnings, and worked into metal items for altars and jewelry. Students can choose one of these motifs to adapt into a design for a copper repoussé plaque or a copper amulet box.

PREPARATION

Before making a copper piece, have students take some time to become familiar with the material and the process of working the metal surface with the tools. They can explore different marks and pressures, turning over the piece back and forth to see the ornamented surface develop. With patience, their confidence and skill will gradually develop as the work progresses.

<u>*The Standard of Victory*</u>
"Attainment of enlightenment"

<u>*The Endless Knot*</u>
"Interrelatedness of all things"

<u>*The Vase*</u>
"Fulfillment of highest aspirations"

<u>*The Golden Fish*</u>
"Freedom from restraint"

Figure 7-10A. Glorious Buddhist emblems. (Used by permission of Newark Museum.)

The Lotus
"Purity and transcendance"

The Umbrella
"Buddha as universal spiritual monarch"

The Wheel of Law
"Buddhist doctrine"

The Conch Shell
"The spoken word"

Figure 7-10B. Glorious Buddhist emblems. (Used by permission of the Newark Museum.)

This experimentation will encourage students to proceed to a complete project. The copper plaque is not difficult; it just requires patience. The amulet box is more intricate, requiring their commitment to more time-consuming and careful craft.

MATERIALS

- 36-gauge copper foil
- scissors
- corrugated cardboard for backing
- pencil, paper, and ballpoint pen
- wooden modeling tools
- a mat on which to work the metal (made by putting folded newspapers into a plastic bag)
- soft cloth
- clear spray fixative

PROCEDURE

1. Select one of the Eight Glorious Buddhist Emblems to adapt into a design inside a flame halo.
2. Work up the sketch until it is resolved.
3. Transfer the drawing to the metal by placing it securely over the metal sheet, and impressing the lines with a ballpoint pen, firmly enough to mark the metal, but not hard enough to tear the paper.
4. Begin the work by pressing the larger areas out, turning the piece over, gradually working back and forth to develop your intended form in more and more refinement of detail. Patience is the key.
5. Leave tabs along the edge to attach the finished piece to a backing.
6. Cut a piece of corrugated cardboard to fit, and bend the metal edges around it, so it can be hung on a wall.
7. Polish the surface of the finished piece gently with a soft cloth.
8. Apply a clear spray coating to protect it.

CONCLUSION

Display all of the plaques together. Discuss the symbolism of the emblems students have used, and have each student write an explanatory caption for his or her artwork. Figure 7–11 shows an actual studio art project.

FOLLOW-UP

Have students research some of the multitudes of Tibetan dieties, and draw more symbolic designs.

CREATIVE WRITING

Write an imaginative interpretation of the flame halo that emanates from images and objects in Tibetan art.

Figure 7-11. Studio art project. Copper repoussé plaque. Flame halo surrounds the vase containing three gems: fulfillment of highest aspirations. (Artwork by Susan Hogan.)

Project 7–5: Making a Copper Repoussé Amulet Box

PREPARATION

To use the patterns given in Figures 7–12A and 7–12B, photocopy the pages as many times as necessary. Students can use one of the Eight Glorious Buddhist Emblems from the previous project, or create their own design idea from the "Follow-Up" research.

MATERIALS

- 36-gauge copper foil
- pencil, paper, and ballpoint pen
- X-acto™ knife or razor blade
- wooden modeling tools
- a mat on which to work the metal (made by putting folded newspapers into a plastic bag)
- a nail
- glue
- ruler
- scissors
- 2-inch copper wire

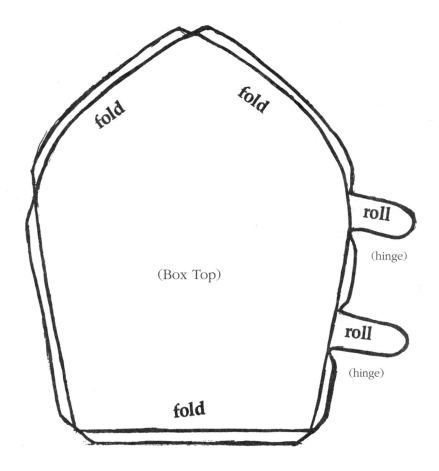

Figure 7-12A. Pattern for top of copper amulet box.

PROCEDURE

1. On the pattern for the front of the box, sketch the designs to emboss on the front.
2. Then transfer the pattern to the metal foil by placing it securely over the metal sheet.
3. Impress the lines with a ballpoint pen, firmly enough to mark the metal, but not hard enough to tear the paper.
4. Then cut out the two pieces of the box very slowly and carefully. This will require patiently bending and smoothing out the copper foil as you go along.
5. To cut the slits in the back of the box for the tabs to be inserted into, use an X-acto™ knife or a new razor blade. **Use caution when working with knives or razors**.
6. To assemble the box, use a small ruler to bend the sides and bottom forward.
7. Insert the tabs into the slits from the outside, then bend the tabs up to hold the box securely together.
8. Insert the tab at the peak inside the matching top slit, and bend it flat.
9. Roll the top strip around a nail to form the hanging loop.
10. Roll the hinges around a nail.

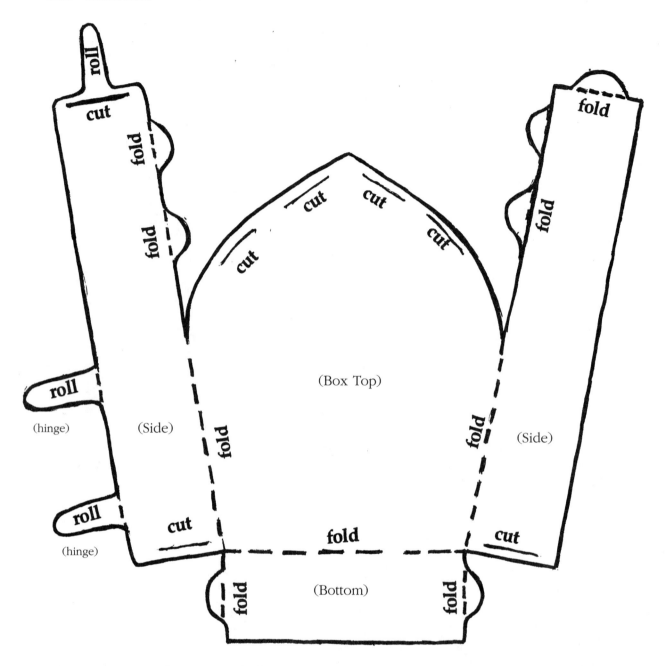

Figure 7-12B. Pattern for copper amulet box.

11. Emboss the top with your design.
12. Roll the top hinges around a nail.
13. Attach the top to the box by putting two pieces of wire through the hinge loops.

CONCLUSION

Suspend the amulet boxes from hanging cords to display them on a wall. Figure 7–13 shows an actual studio art project.

Figure 7-13. Studio art project. Copper amulet box. The two fish are "Glorious Buddhist emblems" symbolizing freedom from restraint. (Artwork by Susan Hogan.)

FOLLOW-UP

Now that students have developed skill in copper repoussé technique, they are prepared to design and make a more personal artwork in embossed metal.

CREATIVE WRITING

Write a story about a magical protective talisman.

Vocabulary Worksheet for Tibet

Look up the definition of each of these words in a dictionary and then use the word in writing a sentence about Tibet. Use a separate sheet of paper for this activity.

amulet box	psyche
asylum	regalia
Chang Thang	reincarnation
consecrated	repoussé
coracles	shamanism
Cultural Revolution	skull drums
dakinis	sky burial
Dalai Lama	steppes
exile	stupas
iconography	tanka
Lhasa	transcendent
nomadic life	verdant
Potala	yak
prayer wheels	

Geography Worksheet for Tibet

Refer to world atlases and travel guides to answer these problems. If you need more space, use the back of this sheet.

- Choose one of these rivers: Mekong, Brahmaputra, Indus, Yangtze. Describe its path from origin to the ocean.

  _____

  _____

- Name the four highest mountains in the Himalayas and give their altitudes.

  _____

  _____

- Identify three cities in Tibet, and research their history, population size, cultural make-up, and attractions for travellers.

  _____

  _____

- Describe the relationship between climate and nomadism.

  _____

  _____

- Find out what kind of mining for metals has been initiated in Tibet in the past two decades.

  _____

  _____

- How is Tibet's international balance of trade calculated, and how would you character-ize it?

  _____

  _____

Geography Worksheet for Tibet (continued)

- Describe the southern border of Tibet. Where is it located, and what countries border Tibet on the south?

  _____

  _____

- Describe the geographic similarities between Tibet and Inner Mongolia.

  _____

  _____

- The Himalayas are still rising higher in altitude. What effect will this have on the climate of Tibet?

  _____

  _____

- Why is travel by automobile or truck in Western Tibet so difficult?

  _____

  _____

Related Assignments for Tibet

1. **Travelogue**. Read guidebooks to present-day Tibet and plan a trip for a specific purpose, such as to study and learn about the culture, art, religion, wildlife, scientific resources, and language.

2. **Adventure stories**. Read Heinrich Harrer and the accounts of other explorers in Tibet.

3. **Ecology**. Find out what the world nature conservancies, particularly Greenpeace, are doing in Tibet. Compare levels of wildlife population between 1900 and 1990. Do the same with the human population. What has affected the numbers of people living in Tibet in recent history?

4. **Human rights**. Research the record of human rights in Tibet since the Chinese took over in 1959. Look at conflicting points of view on how the Tibetan people have been treated. How can we determine what is factual from propaganda?

5. **Biography**
   - Dalai Lama
   - Panchen Lama
   - Milarepa
   - Padmasambava

6. **Topics for further research**
   - nomadic life in central Asia
   - contemporary Tibetan life in exile, in Dharamsala, India, and other cities
   - international trade between Tibe and Western markets

RESOURCES FOR TEACHING

BOOKS

Dalai Lama: Many books by the fourteenth Dalai Lama on the practice of Buddhism are distributed by Potala Publications, 107 E. 31st Street (4th floor), New York, NY 10016. Phone: (212) 213-5010.

Dunham, Carroll and Ian Baker. Photographs by Thomas L. Kelly. *Tibet: Reflections from the Wheel of Life*. New York: Abbeville Press, 1993.

Hyde-Chambers, Fredrick and Audrey. *Tibetan Folk Tales*. Boulder, CO: Shambala, 1981.

Jackson, David P. and Janice A. *Tibetan Thangka Painting, Methods and Materials*. London: Serindia Publications, 1984.

Lipton, Mimi. (ed.). *The Tiger Rugs of Tibet*. London: Thames & Hudson, 1989.

Pal, Pratapaditya. *Tibetan Paintings*. London: Ravi Kumar/Sotheby Publications, 1984.

Reynolds, Valrae. *Tibetan Buddhist Altar*, Newark Museum, 1991. 32 pages, 35 photos: $8.00 from the Newark Museum Shop (address below).

Tibet—A Hidden World, 1905-1935, a postcard book of 30 black and white oversized postcards of scenery and cultural heritage; $9.95 from the Newark Museum Shop (address below).

VIDEOTAPE

"Tibet: The Living Tradition"; three programs on one 55-minute videotape include Tibetan Buddhist Art, Music & Dance, and Tibetan Buddhist Altar, available from The Newark Museum shop (see address below) for $39.95.

PUBLICATIONS

Tibetan Review, published monthly in New Delhi, India

Tricycle, a Buddhist magazine published quarterly

MUSEUM RESOURCES

American Museum of Natural History
79th Street & Central Park West
New York, NY 10024
(212) 769-5100

Seattle Asian Art Museum
1400 E. Prospect St.
Seattle, WA 98112
(206) 625-8901

The Newark Museum
49 Washington Street
P.O. Box 540
Newark, NJ 07101
(201) 596-6550

BIBLIOGRAPHY

Bonavia, David and Magnus Bartlett. *Tibet*. New York: Vendome, 1981.

Booz, Elizabeth B. *Tibet*. (A fascinating look at the Roof of the World, its People, & Culture). Chicago: Passport Books, 1989.

Dalai Lama XIV (Tenzin Gyatso). *Freedom in Exile*. (The autobiography of the Dalai Lama.) New York: HarperCollins, 1990.

Dalai Lama XIV (Tenzin Gyatso). *My Tibet*. Berkeley: University of California Press, 1990.

Dunham, Carroll and Ian Baker. Photographs by Thomas L. Kelly. *Tibet: Reflections from the Wheel of Life*. New York: Abbeville Press, 1993.

Harrer, Heinrich. (trans. by Richard Graves). *Seven Years in Tibet*. New York: J. P. Tarcher, Putnam, 1982.

McCue, Gary. *Trekking in Tibet, A Traveller's Guide*. Seattle: The Mountaineers, 1991.

Reynolds, Valrae, Amy Heller, and Janet Gyatso. *Catalogue of the Newark Museum Tibetan Collection*. Newark, NJ: The Newark Museum, 1986.

Rowell, Galen. *Mountains of the Middle Kingdom*. (Exploring the high peaks of China and Tibet.) San Francisco: Sierra Club, 1983.

Taylor, Chris. *Tibet*. (A Lonely Planet travel survival kit.) Hawthorne, Australia: Lonely Planet, 1995.

SECTION EIGHT
China

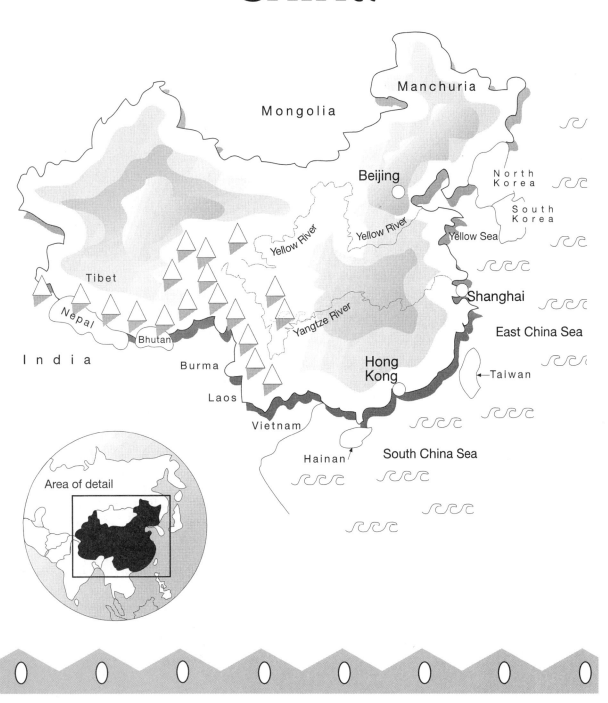

Manchuria

Mongolia

Beijing

North Korea

South Korea

Yellow River

Yellow River

Yellow Sea

Tibet

Shanghai

Nepal

East China Sea

Bhutan

Yangtze River

India

Burma

Hong Kong

Taiwan

Laos

Vietnam

Hainan

South China Sea

Area of detail

A BRIEF HISTORY OF CHINA

The arts of China offer visible evidence of 5,000 years of cultural heritage. Many particular crafts of working with unique materials were invented and developed very far back in Chinese history. Development of basic techniques of pottery, including the use of the wheel, the first spinning and weaving of silk, elaborate bronze casting, the earliest lacquer work, as well as writing with brush and ink, were some of the technical innovations that provided the strong foundation for China's distinctive and masterful artistic traditions to thrive for so many centuries.

These art forms have traditionally been aristocratic—they were luxury items created under the patronage of wealthy rulers and their retinues. Silk, for example, was always produced by peasant women for wealthy patrons, but they could not afford it for their own use. Jade has always been precious, rare and expensive, carved by artisans for the upper classes who could afford to buy uniquely wrought pieces. The formal hierarchical organization of Chinese society, in which the interest of the individual has always been subordinated to tradition, has been an important factor in maintaining support for traditional artistic practices throughout its long history.

The vast majority of Chinese people have always been peasants, very closely connected to the land and the production of food. Throughout their history, the people have experienced periodic cycles of political upheaval and change. In the twentieth century the hegemony of Chinese communism has determined the political power structure of the nation since the communist revolution in 1949. Since the death of Chairman Mao Zedong in 1976, the hard-line economic and social policies of the authoritarian communist government have gradually eased to encourage the increase of material abundance.

When Deng Xiaoping came to power, Mao's ten-year Cultural Revolution gradually came to an end. Mao had formed the Red Guard of young workers and students in 1966, determined to maintain the revolutionary fervor against increasing bureaucratic control of government. He charged the youthful and fanatic Red Guard army with overthrowing the existing party structure and government throughout China. In order to break the power of the intellectual elite, officials, teachers, managers, and scholars were criticized and humiliated. Scholarship and creativity were stifled, education came to a standstill, and economic chaos wasted a decade. The serious disruption of cultural and economic life has been regretted by most Chinese as an extreme political mistake. Now, however, the society is regaining its momentum in an explosion of economic development.

China is now the most populous country in the world, but must provide food, clothing, and housing for all of its people from the mere one-third of the land that is arable and inhabitable. (See Figure 8-1.) The pressures of rapid population expansion have become so intense that family size is now limited by law to one child per married couple. This change in national policy, implemented in 1984, is generally followed by urban dwellers, but is not easily enforced in rural communities, where conservative family traditions resist change and limitation.

Business development and individual initiative are now being encouraged to promote the expansion of the economy. Enterprise zones on the south coast of China have been designated to develop manufacturing and trade for world markets. Western-style advertising is generating consumer attitudes in the Chinese people.

In spite of what seem to be sweeping changes in society, more freedom, and greater Western influence in style, certain Chinese artistic traditions seem to endure. The traditional arts of silk weaving and embroidery, shoemaking, and porcelain and jade sculpture connect

Figure 8-1. Map of China. This is a simplified locator map for quick reference. Students can look up a more detailed map of China in a world atlas.

the best of centuries of cultural development with contemporary products made both for domestic use and for export to world markets.

CHINESE JADE

The Chinese word for jade is *yu*; the same word means precious, pure, and noble. *Yu* also means "stone worthy of carving." The mineral identity of jade is nephrite, or sodium micacite, found in white and a wide range of greens. Jadeite, a harder crystalline stone also always known as jade, has a much wider color range, including brilliant emerald green (from chromium inclusion) as well as yellow, mauve, brown, blue, red, gray, and white.

The remote source of jade is now the Xinjiang Autonomous Region, which was formerly Chinese Turkestan. Deep in central Asia, it was for many centuries a distant hostile territory. The distance and difficulty of obtaining it has contributed to jade's high value and precious status. Jadeite has been obtained from river valleys in Burma since the late eighteenth century, at even greater distance and expense. The precious stones were sometimes used as currency.

Carved jade disks found in tombs from the Shang dynasty (fifteenth century B.C.) are symbolic of heaven and the sun. Carved jade cicadas were placed in the mouths of the dead because they were symbols of resurrection. Early Han rulers had entire burial suits made for themselves out of small jade plaques, because jade was believed to prevent decay. Ceremonial blades, amulets, girdle ornaments, cups, and vessels are other artifacts that have been unearthed from these early times. Stylized forms of animals such as tigers and double-headed dragons show the evolution of more and more elaborate craftsmanship.

Jade mountain carvings have been a recurring form of sculpture in jade since the Ming dynasty. The figure of a hermit on his path through mountains and pine trees to a distant pavilion or hut symbolically expresses the Taoist vision of man contemplating the harmony of nature. (See Figure 8-2.) It is a vision of the world beyond time. This perennial theme, in a constant style and technique, is consistent with the Chinese philosophy of art not as a temporal phenomenon, but as timeless truth.

Small ornaments of jade were habitually worn by the aristocratic classes as part of their costume up to the twentieth century. Jade pendants, belts, scepters, medallions, and hairpins contributed status and elegance to their costuming. The jingling of bells or chimes on belts or girdles expressed happiness and kept evil spirits away.

Jade ornaments and sculpture are customarily created in small workshops of several artisans. Each piece will probably be worked by several sculptors at different stages in its manufacture. First, the outer covering of the stone is cut away to reveal its qualities and variations of color and texture. When the best subject has been selected to coordinate with the shape and color of the jade, the manager of the workshop draws the design on the stone. Completing a work of art in jade is a cooperative process—each carver is a specialist in a particular phase. They do some cutting with different power tools such as drills and saws, but because jade is so exceptionally hard, it must be patiently worn away by grinding with abrasive powder in a very slow and tedious process.

Jade sculptors have always combined their talents to create art work, and did not sign it. Thus, it is very difficult to date jade sculpture. The art remains timeless in the Chinese manner—an art of ancient origin that is still practiced with great delicacy and refinement, to create works along the entire scale of value, from rare and highly valuable luxury items to more ordinary and plentiful pendants, rings, bracelets, and talismans that are widely available and affordable for almost everyone. (See Figure 8-3.)

Project 8-1: Making "Jade" Pendants and Medallions Out of Polymer Clay

Even though the most prized qualities of jade—its hardness, resonance, and the pleasure of its touch—are missing in this simulation, working with polymer clay is an enjoyable way to explore design for jade and to create an imitation.

PREPARATION

Make photocopies of pierced jade medallions from books on the subject, and cut them out to use as preliminary patterns.

MATERIALS

- polymer clay in four colors—metallic green, pale yellow, white, and translucent (4 individual packages of Sculpey III™, for example, should be enough material for 20 students to make a small piece)
- paper, pencils, and scissors

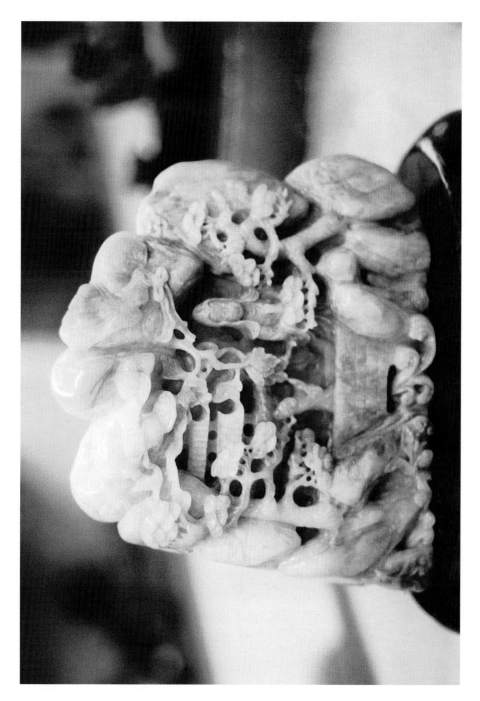

Figure 8-2. In this contemporary jade mountain sculpture, two different nature retreats are carved on either side of the stone. (Courtesy of Jade Garden Arts and Crafts Co.)

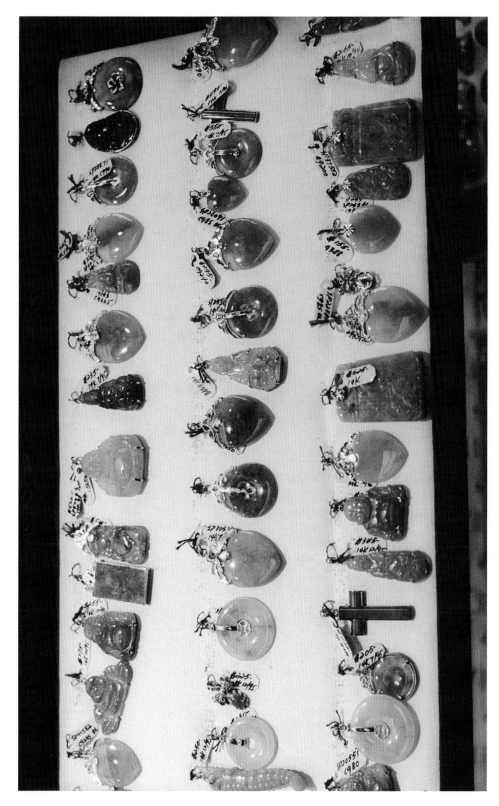

Figure 8-3. A great variety of jade pendants are available in the jewelry shops of Chinatown in New York City.

- modeling tools
- aluminum foil on a pan
- clear gloss varnish
- oven set at 275°

PROCEDURE

1. Mix jade color by combining small amounts of green, white, pale yellow, and translucent and matching the mixture to jade pictured in color reproductions. Although white was most valued to the Chinese, to most non-Chinese, pale green is more identifiable as the color of jade.
2. Prepare your designs by altering the photocopied image of Chinese medallions with a pencil or pen, darkening and simplifying the pierced areas.
3. Cut out the outside shape of the paper design.
4. Press out a thin layer of the mixed polymer clay on smooth paper or plastic.
5. Place the pattern on the clay.
6. Press or cut around the outline. (A toothpick or nail will do as a tool.)
7. Transfer the pierced pattern to clay by pressing on each element.
8. Develop filigree by removing negative areas with a toothpick or dental tool. A metal nail file can also be used.
9. Smooth cut edges as much as possible by rounding the corners with gentle even pressure with the tool.
10. A pendant needs a hole for the chain; a hair clip can be curved by forming it over a roll of aluminum foil while being hardened in the oven.
11. Place on a foil pan to bake to a hard consistency.
12. Bake at 275° for about 40 minutes.
13. When cooled, varnish with clear gloss.

CONCLUSION

Have students making rubbings of the pieces on paper, then assemble a catalog of their new work. Figure 8-4 shows an actual studio art project.

FOLLOW-UP

Look for examples of real jade stones in gem shops and of jade jewelry and other jade objects in Chinese import shops. Compare the look and feel of the genuine substance with the plastic imitation.

CREATIVE WRITING

(*Teacher*: Hand out photocopies of Chinese poems about jade for the students to read aloud.) Write your personal interpretations of the poems.

Figure 8-4. Studio art project. Fake jade pendants, medallions, and hair clasps are made of polymer clay in various shades of green. (Artwork by Beverly Fuchsman, Marguerite Botto, and Susan Hogan.)

CHINESE PORCELAIN

It was the high esteem and value accorded to jade that inspired the Chinese to try to replicate its fine translucence and gloss in ceramic art, and motivated the progressive refinement and purification of the natural clays in the centuries-long development of fine porcelain.

Porcelain is a very fine and durable ceramic ware that is in such wide use today that we take it for granted in our modern world. From our ordinary tableware to our sinks, tubs, and toilets, from electrical insulators and transmitters to jet engines and space capsules this unique product of the earth provides basic amenities for our daily lives on many levels.

Porcelain was first developed by the Chinese from the white kaolin clays and feldspar rock found abundantly in particular river valleys in China. Chinese potters, in the oldest ceramic tradition we know, had also developed kilns to fire at temperatures intense enough to transform the fine white clay into vitreous (glass-like) forms. This remarkable technical achievement evolved gradually over thousands of years, from the Shang Dynasty (1700-1027 B.C.) to the Yuan period (1260-1358 A.D.).

We know that porcelain was traded in the Persian Gulf during the Tang dynasty because shards of it have been found there. The Portuguese finally reached the Chinese port of Canton from Europe and established regular trade in 1554. The porcelain they exported was simply decorated with underglaze blue painting. Dutch ships captured Portuguese cargo to sell in Amsterdam, and the great popularity of Chinese porcelain there, as well as the tea and silk, stimulated the extensive China trade of the seventeenth century.

By the eighteenth century, the English dominated the trade among China, Europe, and America. Millions of porcelain items painted in the standard underglaze blue were exported during that era. Decorative Chinese arts became very fashionable for interior decor, in the prevalent style known as *Chinoiserie* in Europe and America.

Mass production of porcelain ware for thriving trade in international markets is a major industry in China today, as it has been for the past ten centuries. The city of Jing de Zhen, in Jiangxi Province, has been a center of pottery production since early Ming times. In the large factories here, many talented artisans of the region make a living producing and painting distinctive ceramic ware both for domestic Chinese use and for export. (See Figure 8-5.) The city of Luoyang in Hunan province has been producing celadon-glazed ware in quantity since porcelain was developed many centuries ago.

Figure 8-5. Blue and white Chinese porcelain is for sale in import shops. (Courtesy of Pier 1 Imports.)

Pilgrim bottles were brought into China by travellers crossing the immense Asian deserts along the Silk Road from the eastern Mediterranean—either bearing holy water from shrines or carrying water for drinking. This flask type became part of the repertoire of Tang ceramicists. (See Figure 8-6.) The use of pilgrim bottles in China was decorative and ceremonial rather than as practical water carriers of other cultures.

Figure 8-6. This porcelain pilgrim bottle with underglaze blue design of leaves and flowers was made in the 18th century. (Photograph by Armen. Collection of the Newark Museum, Newark, New Jersey. Jaehne Collection, 1941.)

Project 8-2: Making a Chinese Moon Flask

PREPARATION

Look up the vast panorama of Chinese pottery in art books, and find pictures of blue and white china (traditional motifs) as resources. List categories of decoration, and have students choose a style of decoration for their painting on a pot in blue and white style.

MATERIALS

- low-fire white clay, cone 06
- uncoated paper plates or wooden salad bowls, about 4- to 6-inch diameter
- electric kiln
- clay modeling tools
- 1-inch wooden dowel or round brush handle
- surface for wedging and kneading
- plastic bags for slow drying
- pencil
- blue underglaze and brushes
- gloss glaze in a spray bottle, water

PROCEDURE

1. Wedge a lump of clay.
2. Press a thin layer of clay into two uncoated paper plates or small wooden bowls.
3. Smooth the surface and the edges.
4. Let the clay stiffen enough to pull away from the sides of the mold.
5. Use slip to adhere the two halves together.
6. Smooth the seam, and set this hollow form aside.
7. Roll out a thin slab to use for the pedestal, neck, and handles.
8. Make a pedestal by forming a flared tube, about 1-1/2 inches high, on which to set the bottle. Cut a curve to fit the bottom of the bottle, and attach the two pieces with slip.
9. Make the neck by forming a slab over a 1-inch round form.
10. Cut a round hole in the top of the bottle for the neck.
11. Insert the neck into the hollow bottle, using slip to attach it firmly.
12. Cut matching handles out of the clay slab and attach them to the bottle with slip at the juncture of the bottle and neck.
13. Smooth the seams and surfaces.
14. Dry slowly by covering loosely with a plastic bag.
15. When the bottle is dry, use a pencil to sketch your design onto the surfaces. Handle greenware with great care.
16. Paint the design with blue underglaze.

17. Bisque fire the underglazed flasks to cone 06.

18. Use a spray bottle to apply gloss glaze—diluted 50% with water—over the painting.

19. Glaze fire the moon flasks to cone 06.

CONCLUSION

Have students arrange a display of these bottles. Figure 8-7 shows an actual studio art project.

Figure 8-7. Studio art project. Moon flask made of white clay pressed into molds, and painted with underglaze blue in designs inspired by Chinese ceramics. (Artwork by Susan Hogan.)

FOLLOW-UP

Take a field trip to a china shop, gift shop, or antique shop to seek out Chinese-influenced designs in pottery and dinnerware. Look for examples of blue-willow ware and antique flow blue plates, and find out what they are worth.

CREATIVE WRITING

Write about taking the pilgrim flasks on an imaginary journey along the Silk Road from China into western Asia and on to the Middle East.

CHINESE PAGODAS

The pagoda structure is a distinctive feature of the Chinese landscape. A pagoda is an identifying landmark, an uplifting influence and symbol of devotion that evolved into this unique tower form throughout many centuries. Wherever they are situated in the countryside, pagodas have become a center of local legends and tutelary dieties, exercising their beneficial protective influence.

During the Han Dynasty (206 B.C. to 220 A.D.), a period of peace and consolidation in the turbulent timeline of China, clay models of wooden palaces and houses were placed in the tombs to make the dead feel at home. (See Figure 8-8.) These structures are typical of domestic life in the first century B.C.

Figure 8-8. Han Dynasty pavilion of ceramic, includes figures and animals. (Photograph by Witt. Collection of the Newark Museum, Newark, New Jersey. Jaehne Collection, 1939.)

The little models of watchtowers, or narrow multi-storied dwellings, show their origin in timber framework construction, known as post and beam. The form is stacked open rooms, like pavilions with balconies. The roof styles depict typical roof construction: the tubular ceramic tile for roofing was already in wide useage. The watchtowers that are depicted in Han terra cottas appear to be the forerunners of the Buddhist pagoda.

When Buddhism was brought to China from India in the first century A.D., the stupa, or temple, was combined with the Chinese tower to develop a unique Chinese-style temple. The pagoda has been a distinctive image expressing Chinese identity in painting, pottery, and city architecture for centuries. They have always been landmarks for Chinese travelers and still are tourist destinations in China.

The famous Wild Goose pagoda in ChangAn dates back to 701-705 A.D.. It is 190 feet high and considered a national treasure. Most towers and pagodas, which were built of wood, have not lasted through time, but we can infer how they were constructed and how they looked from the Han tomb sculptures. Another source of information are some of the surviving ancient temple structures of Japan that were built as virtually exact copies of Chinese-style pagodas.

Project 8-3: Building a Model Watchtower Out of Clay

PREPARATION

Most picture books on the arts of China have at least one or two pictures of Han burial terra cottas. Museum publications are another source of visual information about the myriad variations of this type of structure that have been unearthed from Han times.

MATERIALS

- low-fire white clay, cone 06
- rolling pin or large dowel to roll out slabs
- paper, pencil, ruler

- electric kiln
- cloay modeling tools

PROCEDURE

1. Sketch a series of rooms in the Han style that could be stacked to build a miniature tower.
2. Draw your final design to scale.
3. Use the rectangular elements of your sketch for patterns to cut out clay sides of the "boxes"/rooms.
4. Construct a series of three slab boxes of clay, diminishing in size.
5. The clay will need to stiffen a bit by drying somewhat before the three rooms can be stacked and "glued" together with thick slip. Support the hollow interiors with crushed paper.
6. Construct mini-roofs, and add railings and lattice work as decorative elements.
7. Dry the clay pieces slowly and thoroughly before firing to cone 06.

CONCLUSION

Display the finished pieces as a group and ask the students to discuss the process and results. Figure 8-9 shows an actual studio art project.

Figure 8-9. Studio art project. Three rectangular "boxes" of clay are pierced with openings, stacked with balconies and curved roofs—all "glued" firmly together with slip. (Artwork by Susan Hogan.)

FOLLOW-UP

- Students can make small figures and animals to populate their clay models.
- Have each student select one particular historical pagoda or other example of architecture in China on which to give a report.

CREATIVE WRITING

Imagine you are a European traveller to China on a ship in the sixteenth century. Describe the approach to the shores of this foreign land. What would you see? feel? imagine? anticipate?

CHINESE COSTUMES

For the long 5,000-year history of Chinese civilization, costume has always been a brilliant feature, and closely related to politics, economics, culture, and all of the arts. We can see visible evidence of historical styles in pottery figurines, frescoes, sculptures, stone carvings, and famous paintings from all eras.

Handicrafts began to develop in the matriarchal communities between 4000 B.C. and 3000 B.C. when plant fibers were spun into thread and woven into cloth. By the time of the Shang Dynasty (1480-1122 B.C.), the art of silk weaving had been mastered, and embroidery and cloth-dying crafts were refined into beautiful art forms that extended for thousands of years. During the succeeding dynasties—the Xia, Shang, and Zhou—a system of dress was developed to enable rulers to identify status and demonstrate authority. By codifying costumes into a specific ranking system, a visible social hierarchy was established, and social order was highly controlled.

Colors were specified for each level, and strict rules applied to shoe colors. Costumes bore symbolic motifs as well. In the Ming Dynasty (1368-1644 A.D.), badges of rank were required to be worn stitched to the breast of long overdresses. For the empresses, there were detailed specifications for the dress for each ceremonial occasion, and for aristocratic women of the court, there were regulations for each rank. The Sumptuary Laws controlled every aspect of dress, and any variation from these extremely detailed rules—in material, color, pattern, or measurement of garments—was strictly prohibited.

Variations in headgear indicated a person's social status. The hairstyle for women was always a highly coiled bun, which became more and more elaborate, ornamented, and artificial throughout the centuries.

These strict styles that were established in the early dynasties, from about 150 B.C. onward, had a long life. Chinese emperors wore similar elaborate robes to preside over important ceremonies of state for over 2,000 years, until the fall of the Qing Dynasty in the early twentieth century. Similarly, women continued to wear the jacket and skirt in daily life for more than 2,000 years. (See Figure 8-10.) It wasn't until the Revolution of 1911 that identification of social status by costume and headgear was abolished, and the more egalitarian fashions of Western (foreign) custom were called for. Shanghai was the port city for trade with the West, and became the fashion center of the nation.

China has been dominant in the world silk trade for more than 2,000 years, and even today silk clothing made in China is widely distributed in Western markets. Silkworm culture was traditionally handled by women, who fed the worms mulberry leaves. Silkworms were cultivated in stacks of trays like shelves. The cocoons were boiled in cauldrons to loosen the thread to be drawn into filaments. Then the silk threads were twisted together, and silk cloth woven on large looms.

Today silk manufacture is still a substantial industry in China. No longer a luxury for aristocrats only, silk textiles and clothing are exported at very moderate prices for a mass market. Known as "silk city," the city of Hangzhou on the coast south of Shanghai is a distinctive location for the production of silk, satins, brocades, silk parasols, and handicraft items.

Figure 8-10. Portrait of a Civil Officer's Wife (hanging scroll, late 19th century China) in ink and color on paper. Women of the upper class wore the same robe type and badge as their husbands until the revolution in 1911. On her rank badge, the flycatcher denotes the ninth civil rank, and a glimpse of the imperial mountain. Under her robe she wears a pleated skirt with the dragon, mountain, and sea pattern. The headdress bears a dense cluster of pearls, jade, and kingfisher feather-covered metal ornaments in the form of auspicious birds, flowers, and emblems. (Photograph by Sarah Wells. Collection of the Newark Museum, Newark, New Jersey. Gift of Cornelia Susack, 1976.)

Project 8-4: Making a Fabric Collage of Historical Chinese Costumes

PREPARATION

Gather visual historical resources for design reference: books of Chinese painting, ceramics, and sculpture that have clear pictures. (See Figure 8-11.)

Figure 8-11. Three padded paper dolls of silk on paper, made in Canton, China, in the 1920s show Chinese fashion of that time. (Photograph by Sarah Wells. Collection of the Newark Museum, Newark, New Jersey. Gift of C. W. Howard, Canton Christian College, Canton, China, 1925.)

MATERIALS

- fashion figures clipped from newspapers and magazines
- scissors
- paper and pencils
- straight pins
- glue sticks or gel medium or white glue
- scraps of fabric of different colors, textures, and patterns (old silk clothing, old neckties, sample books for decorator fabrics are good if you can get expired ones from dealers)

PROCEDURE

1. Select examples of Chinese art from visual resources.
2. Cut out the fashion figure into a silhouette.
3. Trace around it (like a paper doll) on paper.
4. Sketch the design of the Chinese costume on the "paper doll."
5. Cut out the paper costume pieces to use as a pattern.
6. Place the pattern pieces on selected fabric.
7. Pin with straight pins, and cut fabric according to patterns.
8. Cut paper doll out of fabric, too.
9. Combine the figure and costume on a background cloth.
10. Adhere with gel medium, white glue, or glue stick.

CONCLUSION

Arrange the students' costume collages in chronological order to show a vignette of history of culture and social custom in China. Figure 8-12 shows an actual studio art project.

Figure 8-12. Studio art project. Fabric collages are interpretations of Chinese paintings of robed aristocrats. (Artwork by Marguerite Botto and Beverly Fuchsman.)

- By using many of these "paper dolls" for costume design, students can construct a collage scene of figures from different eras in Chinese history.
- Students could also translate a Chinese work of art into a fabric picture.

CREATIVE WRITING

Write a description of the costumed characters in their historical situation and social role.

CHINESE SHOES OF COTTON CLOTH

As we have seen, shoes have been a clear indicator of status throughout Chinese history, traditionally designated by costume codes for the aristocratic classes of scholars, rulers, and bureaucrats, who followed strict ranking rules for footwear. Workers and peasants, however, have always worn handmade cotton shoes. The soles are formed of many layers of cotton cloth stitched together in the prescribed fashion of an archetypal handicraft. In the peasant class, shoemaking has always been an important skill for a wife to have, because the cotton shoes wear out fairly quickly. Constantly replacing the shoes of everyone in the family turns out to be a fairly steady occupation.

Cotton has traditionally been the cloth of the ordinary citizen, the peasant, worker, or tradesperson. Cotton grows more easily than other cloth fibers in the harsh dry land of northern China. Even though silk was produced by peasant women, it was all for sale or trade—they couldn't afford to use it themselves. Padded cotton clothing has traditionally been made and worn by the working classes of China.

Mothers and grandmothers are still stitching clothing for the children, as they always have. They traditionally make tiger shoes for the kids, along with tiger collars, tiger hats, and tiger pillows. The tiger image protects the child from harm. Other talismans against evil spirits or bad luck embroidered onto clothes or appliquéd onto quilts like the one shown in Figure 8-14 are poisonous insects (scorpions, spiders, and types of caterpillars) and frogs. Bats are emblems of happiness, and are also seen embroidered on collars and hats for children. The embellishment with embroidery is seen as a practical aspect of the work—to insure protection and happiness.

Project 8-5: Making Appliquéd Slippers

PREPARATION

Collect and sketch pictures of Chinese talismans for good luck: the bat, the tiger, Shou, butterfly, and the poisionous insects: spider, caterpillar, scorpion, etc., are some examples of a large range of available symbols. (See Figure 8-13.)

MATERIALS

- paper and pencil
- cloth (for example: felt, canvas, velour, denim)

Figure 8-13. Tiger shoes are traditionally made for small children by mothers and grandmothers. (Courtesy of Virginia Cornue.)

- cardboard for insoles
- hand stapler
- double-fold bias tape
- iron-on adhesive
- scissors
- markers
- chalk
- iron
- trim items (beads, stars, sequins)
- acrylic gel medium

PROCEDURE

1. The first step in making a pattern for the sole is to trace the outline of your foot on paper.
2. Develop the pattern by drawing a *slightly* larger line around the foot outline, and smoothing it out.
3. Make a pattern for the slipper top by using the pattern for the bottom, and tapering it out 1 1/2 to 2 inches on each side as shown in Figure 8-15.
4. For the slipper sole, cut 3 layers for each one as follows: for bottom, use canvas or heavy upholstery fabric; for middle layer, use thin cardboard; for inside layer, use velour or denim.
5. Tack together all three layers of each sole using the hand stapler.
6. Cut slipper tops by tracing around the pattern with chalk (be sure pattern is reversed); then cut out the cloth with scissors.

Figure 8-14. Folk art quilt made in rural China uses dragons, pandas, cats, frogs, scorpions, and snakes, worked in embroidery, appliqué, and trapunto. (Courtesy of Virginia Cornue.)

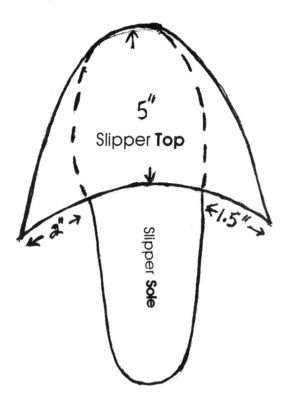

Figure 8-15. Slipper pattern.

7. Make paper cutouts of various animals, insects, birds, butterflies, spiders. Then select a group of appliqué designs you like best.

8. Adhere iron-on adhesive to small cloth pieces to be used as appliqué with a warm iron. **Handle the warm iron carefully!**

9. Placing the emblems of good fortune and protection on the colored fabric, trace around them with a marking pen or pencil, and cut them out.

10. Apply cut fabric designs to the slippers before you put the top and sole together. Press them on with a warm iron.

11. Place the slipper parts—the top and sole—together, and staple the edges together close to the edge, spacing staples 1/4 inch apart all around the sole. (This can also be stitched, but stapling is fast and easy.)

12. Cover the exposed seam by gluing double-fold bias tape all the way around the slipper edge. Cut neatly at the joint. For adhesive, use acrylic gel medium: it is easy to handle, flexible, and easy to rinse off the extra.

CONCLUSION

Have students arrange an informative display of all the slippers, including descriptive captions about the appliqué symbols. See Figure 8-16 for an actual studio art project.

FOLLOW-UP

Students can design and make more fanciful and personally expressive shoes, inventing them as sculpture instead of functional forms.

CREATIVE WRITING

Write a tale about shoes that determine the wearer's status.

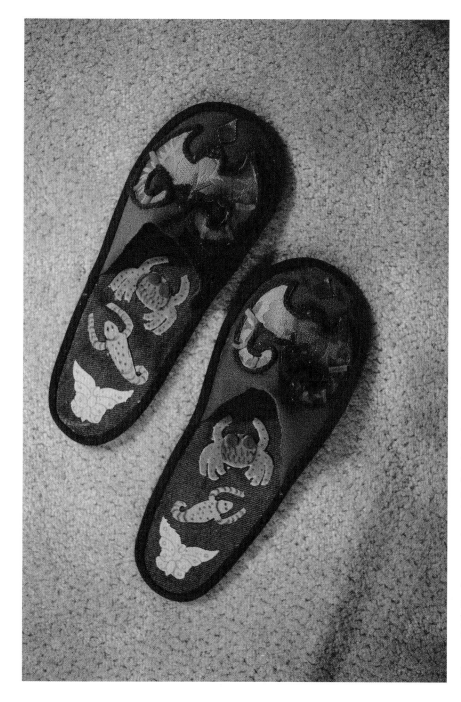

Figure 8-16. Studio art project. Colorful cloth slippers are custom-made for fit, and covered with beneficial symbols: spiders, scorpions, bats, and butterflies. (Artwork by Susan Hogan.)

Name _____ Date _____

Vocabulary Worksheet for China

Look up the following vocabulary words in a dictionary, write the definition, and then use the word in a sentence about China. Use a separate sheet of paper for this activity.

amenities	literati
appliqué	populous
arable	porcelain
chinoiserie	rank badges
cocoons	Red Guard
egalitarian	repertoire
flask	Shang Dynasty
hegemony	silk
hierarchy	slip
immortals	Sumptuary Laws
jade mountains	talisman
jadeite	Taoist
kaolin	terra cottas
lacquer	translucence
lattice	vitreous

Geography Worksheet for China

Find the answers to these problems in world atlases and encyclopedias. Use the back of this sheet if you need more space.

- Compare the physical features of China's geographic situation with those of the United States.

  _____

  _____

- Describe the path of the Yellow River, from its source to the sea.

  _____

  _____

- Where in China would you think that climatic features enable three annual crops of rice to be grown?

  _____

  _____

- Locate the Three Gorges area on a map and describe the towns and archaeological sites that would be swallowed up when the proposed hydroelectric dam is built.

  _____

  _____

- Identify China's Autonomous Regions and find out their distinguishing characteristics.

  _____

  _____

- The Great Wall of China is the only man-made structure visible from outer space. Where, when, and why was it built?

  _____

  _____

Geography Worksheet for China (continued)

- Plan a sea voyage along one section of the 18,000 miles of Chinese coastline. List the provinces, cities, and regions you would visit and describe them.

  _____

  _____

- Locate Shanghai, China's largest city, and report on its economic, geographic, and social statistics.

  _____

  _____

- Both Manchuria and Mongolia, located to the north of central China, were origins of conquering peoples in China's history. Sketch schematic maps of the territory that was controlled by each of these nations during the time they dominated China in the past.

- Choose one province of China to study. Write a report on its climate, terrain, resources, and patterns of habitation.

Related Assignments for China

1. **Current Events**. Follow the news about the GATT treaty between the U.S. and the nations of Asia. List the major points of agreement, and the controversy sparked by this treaty.

2. **Human Rights**. What happened at Tianenman Square in Beijing in 1989?

3. **Biography**
   - Kublai Khan
   - Empress Dowager Cixi
   - Chiang Kai-shek
   - Marco Polo
   - Sun Yat-sen
   - Emperor Puyi
   - Zhou Enlai
   - Deng Xiaoping

4. **Ecology**. Research the natural habitat of panda bears and find out why they are an endangered species.

5. **Environment**. Study the development of the Three Gorges hydroelectric project in news reports. What is the controversy surrounding the building of this huge dam? What will the results be, both positive and negative?

6. **Art History**
   - Chinese ink painting
   - Terra cotta warriors at Xi'an
   - Lacquer art

7. **Modern history**. Study the history of Chinese Communism under Mao Zedong from the revolution in 1949 until the death of Mao in 1976.

8. **Timeline**. Make a timeline of the 5,000 years of Chinese dynasties, and illustrate it with drawings or collage. (See Turkey's Project 1-2 for a description of a timeline painting project).

9. **Economics**. Follow the international art market by reading about the Hong Kong art auctions in Asian art magazines. Translate the prices into Chinese currency, Hong Kong dollars, and U.S. dollars at current rates of exchange.

RESOURCES FOR TEACHING

BOOKS

Hearn, Maxwell K. *Splendors of Imperial China, Treasures from the National Palace Museum, Taipei*. New York: Rizzoli, 1996.

Hermann, Albert. *An Historical Atlas of China*. Chicago: Aldine Publishing Co., 1966.

Schwob, Pierre (ed.). *Great Documents of the World, Milestones of Human Thought*. Maidenhead, England: McGraw-Hill, 1977 (Includes original philosophies of Confucius, Lao-Tse, and Buddha, as well as excerpts from Saint Paul, Gandhi, and the Koran).

Zhou, Xun and Chunming Gao. *Five Thousand Years of Chinese Costume*. Hong Kong and San Francisco: China Books, 1987.

VIDEOTAPES

China: The Mandate of Heaven, in the Legacy series produced by Maryland Public Television and Central Independent Television, UK, 1991.

Discovering China and Tibet, "Video Visits" International Video Network, 1988.

Heart of the Dragon, Public Broadcasting Service, 1986 (series of twelve programs narrated by Robert MacNeil and Jim Lehrer).

PERIODICALS

Arts of Asia, published bi-monthly by Arts of Asia Publications, Ltd., 1309 Kowloon Center, 29-39 Ashley Road, Kowloon, Hong Kong, China. Phone: 23762228.

BOOKSTORE

The Asia Society Bookstore
795 Park Avenue
New York, NY 10021
(212) 288-6400

BIBLIOGRAPHY

Atterbury, Paul (ed.). *The History of Porcelain*. New York: William Morrow & Co., 1982.

Berliner, NancyZeng. *Chinese Folk Art*. Boston: Little, Brown and Co., A NY Graphic Society Book, 1986.

Hartman, Joan M. *Chinese Jade of Five Centuries*. Rutland, VT: Charles E. Tuttle, 1969.

Smith, Bradley and Wan-go Weng. *China, A History in Art*. New York: Harper & Row, no date.

Sullivan, Michael. *The Arts of China*. Berkeley: University of California Press, 1984.

The Contemporary Atlas of China. London: Weidenfeld and Nicolson, 1988.

Willetts, William. *Foundations of Chinese Art*. London: Thames and Hudson, 1965.

Zhou, Xun and Chunming, Gao. *Five Thousand Years of Chinese Costume*. Hong Kong and San Francisco: China Books, 1987.

NOTES

NOTES

NOTES

NOTES